TAKILMA TALES

TAKILMA TALES

THE HIPPIE HISTORY OF TAKILMA, OREGON

SUSANNE KINDI FAHRNKOPF

AuthorHouse™ LLC
1663 Liberty Drive
Bloomington, IN 47403
www.authorhouse.com
Phone: 1-800-839-8640

Published by AuthorHouse   01/09/2014

ISBN: 978-1-4918-4497-7 (sc)
ISBN: 978-1-4918-4496-0 (e)

Library of Congress Control Number: 2013923199

TABLE OF CONTENTS

Part 1 The Early History of Takilma, Oregon-The Natives 1

Part 2 The Early History of Takilma, Oregon-Mining and Logging 5

Part 3 The Beginnings of a Movement 11

Part 4 The first Hippies arrive 19

Part 5 Why Did They Come? 27

Part 6 The Old Cook Ranch 33

Part 7 The Takilma Forge and Stories from Jim 41

Part 8 The Takilma People's Clinic 49

Part 9 The Communes 59

Part 10 Crimes, Protests and Problems in the early years 71

Part 11 Unusual People in the Early Days 79

Part 12 The Takilma Community Building 91

Part 13 The Longwood Fire of 1987 99

Part 14 The Out n About Treehouse Resort 105

Part 15 Making Dreams Come True 113

Part 16 Music in Takilma 125

Part 17 Clean up Challenges 135

Part 18 Solutions and Economic Development 143

Part 19 The Environmental Years in Takilma (Part 1) 149

Part 20 The Environmental Years in Takilma-
(Part 2) 157
Part 21 The Hippies of Takilma—Looking to
the Future 165

Conclusion and Comments 177
Poem by Kindi Fahrnkopf: Into The Mystic 181
List of References 185
About the author 187

DEDICATED TO THE COMMUNITY
OF TAKILMA, WHICH IS AN
EXTRAORDINARY PLACE.

PART 1

The Early History of Takilma, Oregon-The Natives

The history of Takilma is a long story of the "Five Waves" of human habitation which existed there beginning with the Native Americans of the Rogue-Takelma Tribe. Their stories say Takelma was actually named "Dagelma," meaning dragonfly. Col. Draper changed it to Takilma in 1902. The remote forested canyon leading into the botanically rich Siskiyou Mountains was used mostly in warm months as a hunting and gathering area for the partially nomadic tribes. The Takelma village, closer to the present day Jump-Off Joe Creek, was home to a tribe led by Chief Jack "Tolt-nys" Harney. He and brothers Lympe and Tecumtum and their families were among the tribes forced into removal from their homelands. After a skirmish at Agness on the Rogue River, where Lympe had retreated, his following of about 30 natives were killed, in what was to later be called one of the "Rogue Indian Battles."

Col. Buchanan asked for a council with the leaders and promised them if they moved to the reservation they could return to their homelands after four years. Tecumtum did not believe him and resisted capture in the last battle at Big Bend. After being rounded up in an area near Table Rock, the Takelma Indians were forced to march 200 miles north along the coast in the cold fall months of 1856, to reach the land designated for them; a reservation at Siletz, Oregon. This "Trail of Tears" is recognized as one of the worst crimes in Oregon history, and coincided with the Gold Rush.

Chief George "Olhatha" Harney was the grandfather of Agnes Baker Pilgrim, who grew up on the reservation of the Confederated Tribes of Siletz. In 1974 Agnes moved back to southern Oregon and worked at the United Indian Lodge in Crescent City, as a counselor. She married and raised a family of six children over the years, and earned a degree in Psychology from Southern Oregon Community College. She became involved at that time in helping people with social and environmental issues which were coming to light.

She became an activist and advocate for the Earth and even posed for a picture with the entire community of Takilma in 1994. Many of the people at the time felt quite honored that she had come back to her homeland, and have worked with her since then on many issues in and around the Siskiyou Region. One of the first projects was supporting Agnes in her revival of an ancient Takelma ceremony which welcomes the returning salmon back each spring. Tao-why-wee, Agnes' Native American name, organized the annual Salmon Ceremony on the Rogue and Applegate Rivers, in which all people were invited to participate, and to thank the Creator for the rivers of pure water and the salmon beings which sustained them all year long.

In the year 1999, Grandmother Agnes worked with others to secure a grant to build a traditional Pit House dwelling behind the historic Naucke House at the Kerbyville Museum. People donated some logs to build it with, but they were so knotty that they had to mill them with a portable sawmill to construct the house. Otherwise it was constructed in the traditional way with a fire pit in the middle and a smoke hole at the top. By the year 2000 it was finished and a ceremony to dedicate it was held. Grandma Agnes said it made her happy to sit beside the simple dwelling which was a replica of what her people lived in. She pointed to the painted medicine wheel of a dragonfly, which decorated the outside. She said, "My people believed that they were the transformer, which meant that when they died and went to the Star Nations that they came back as dragonflies."

Grandmother Agnes became a spiritual leader and respected elder over the years. She became well loved by the people of Takilma, who had formed an alliance with her. Grandmother Agnes' spiritual path led her to help create a group called the International Council of 13 Indigenous Grandmothers. They "represent a global alliance of prayer, education and healing for Mother Earth, all her inhabitants and all her children for the next seven generations." Since then, the group has been traveling the world advocating for peace and solutions to today's problems. With courage and compassion they have worked to change things. They have met with the Dalai Lama of Tibet and brought wisdom to people's awareness all over the world. The leadership and support of Grandmother Agnes Pilgrim seems to have inspired a connection that the hippie's of the back-to-the-land movement felt for the Native Americans. For more information on the oldest living survivor of the Rogue-Takelma Indians please see www.agnesbakerpilgrim.org

The Community of Takilma in 1994 with honored guest Grandmother Agnes-Baker-Pilgrim Photo by Jim Shames.

PART 2

The Early History of Takilma, Oregon-Mining and Logging

After the Indian's were removed, three more waves of people came to take from the land whatever they could take. First the Gold Rush of the 1850's swept over Southern Oregon, with emigrating parties of miners coming into the region from both California and the Willamette Valley, adding to a small population of widely scattered farms in the Rogue Valley. The region would also have coastal access from Crescent City bringing people in who started Sailor's Diggins. After gold strikes were made in 1851, the boomtown of Waldo sprang up and grew to be home to over 2,500 people, and by 1856 was a thriving town, including a small "China Town," home to over 1,500 Chinese workers. These frenzied miners came by the thousands to scour the hills and valleys of the undisturbed landscape for gold nuggets. With short-sighted greed they ruined riverbeds, valleys, creeks, dug canals and sluiced and drained away millions of tons of topsoil, trees and plant life. When several of the buildings in Waldo burned down they ended their path of destruction by mining out the topsoil of the town with a giant plume of water diverted from the river. Nothing is left of the "Ghost Town" of Waldo except a few scattered old cemeteries, one of which is in Allen Gulch and a few old fruit trees. Legend has it that there are still ghosts above the old cemetery and from the accounts of a miner's wife, shrieking and moaning could be heard and lanterns could be seen flickering through the trees at night.

When copper was discovered in Takilma, first in 1860 and then in 1900, it would draw mine speculators and investors to get enough ore for the country's industrial needs. They built a mine and smelter on the Queen of Bronze Mine on Hope Mountain. This was owned by a Mr. Charles Tutt from 1903-1915. A contract had been signed with Col. John Draper to produce 1,000 tons of copper. By 1904 the smelter was operating at full capacity, and having trouble finding enough willing workers. By 1915 it had produced over 35,000 tons of copper ore. The copper ore was hauled by mule teams from Takilma to a railroad stop of the Crescent City & Oregon Coast Railway at the bottom of Hays Hill. Coal was loaded in the backhaul to fuel the smelter. The round trip took 24 hours. The train station at the bottom of Hays Hill was known as the "Love Station" after its owner James Love. Later the mine was sold and by 1930 the price of copper was so low the smelter was dismantled and the metal recycled. What remained was thrown into the back fill of Lake Shasta. There were few laws to govern the miners, yet their own rules stated that if a claim lay un-worked for

5 days, it was claimable by another, so thereby mining was a way of life which was inherently temporary. Miners just seemed to borrow the land, and leave it when they were done, for another to come and claim it. Several stories of people finding gold on a claim that had been abandoned were found, including the 17 pound nugget found by Mattie Collins in the root ball of a downed tree beside Althouse Creek.

In the 1930's people were fleeing from the Depression and coming west on a great migration similar to the settlers coming west on the Oregon Trail. Many of them came to the Rogue and Illinois Valleys and moved into the small towns and cities, farms and ranches, leftover from earlier times. A few even trickled out to Takilma, where there was a small store, post office, and a boarding house, up until about 1918. These emigrants found jobs as loggers working for the areas many small sawmills. They cut the valley's immense store of ponderosa and sugar pine. By the late 50's the valley was "logged out", and most of the mills closed. Early accounts tell of a time when the Takilma valley was planted with irrigated row crops. They also tell of a rich, fertile valley with abundant water and trees where ranches, farms and dairies flourished. The Homestead Act allowed many people to claim free land. The daughter of one of the early settlers, Ruth Pfefferle's family owned land on Takilma Road. She took an interest in writing and in her early years knew Curly Baird who owned the Post Office and small store in downtown Takilma. In her later years, she became the town historian and wrote a book called "Golden Days and Pioneer Ways," which has much more information on that time period in Takilma.

The largest house in Takilma at the time was known as the boarding house, and had been built by G.B. Fife and later finished by Ole Valens, a Swedish immigrant. John and Mary Valens, his children and many other relatives of the Valens family had welcomed boarders for decades, but it ended up being the home of a woman by the name of Mrs. Heatherbee in the 1970's. She seemed to have fallen on hard times trying to raise six children there and the State was going to take her kids away. She was desperate to leave and sold it to Dred Mikal in very poor condition around 1976. So it happened that the "boarding house" was purchased by a hippie and is still standing.

Gary S., who lived at his parent's ranch on Sauer's Flat in Kerby, remembers coming to Takilma during his teenage years with his family to run their cattle up into the mountains. He recalled that they would, "Drive em up in the mountains to fatten them on the rich grasses, and spend the whole summer up there." Gary remembered when "They would take a wagon to the old Holland Grange hall, and ride it back after the dance, so they could do their chores in the morning. Everybody got together on the weekends for potlucks. I knew everybody back then."

Being a local boy, whose family were among the earliest settlers of the Illinois Valley, Gary still found a lot to like about Takilma in the 60's and 70's. He said, "I was more into that culture than I was into the redneck culture. Lots of people were migrating up here then and it was crazy. I loved Takilma. It was the place to be at the time. Everybody had long hair and nick names, and everybody wanted to move to the mountains and get their heads together. It was a movement." Gary remembers living in a small cabin in Allen Gulch, during a period when he was roughing it, but after that he enlisted in the military and went to Vietnam. When he came home he married and started a family of his own.

The Town of Waldo in 1880. Photo
courtesy of Dennis H. Strayer.

THE TAKILMA SMELTING COMPANY

The Takilma Smelting Co. in 1910, a copper
mine on Hope Mountain owned by Mr Charles
Tutt. Photo courtesy of Greg Walter

PART 3

The Beginnings of a Movement

The hippies of the Illinois Valley came to Takilma, and to a lesser extent other small towns like Selma and O'Brien, during the "back to the land movement" which started during the late 60's and early 70's, yet still continued to grow well into the 80's. The hippie movement got started with the anti-war and anti-nuclear protests, and was fueled by young people of the baby-boomer generation who were fed-up with the corporate-controlled society and the strict morals and rules of their parents. They did not want to conform to society's pressure to fit-in, cut their hair and get a job. Many were affluent, college-educated, middle-class kids, just searching for a deeper spiritual meaning in life.

What is the definition of a "hippie"? Well this of course depends on your viewpoint, but for the purposes of this book, it means someone who is hip, conscious, groovy and cool. It means someone who was born between 1940 and 1965; the liberal, progressive generation who experienced immense changes in the world and responded accordingly. One author, Marilyn Ferguson of *The Aquarian Conspiracy*, described the counter-culture movement as "a collective paradigm shift" and one which includes personal and social transformation. Many times in the history of man you see these characteristics; men wore long hair and people migrated to a new land in search of a better life. This trend is nothing new; it has happened many times since the fall of Rome and the subsequent settling of rural Europe.

One man, Thor Heyerdahl, called himself "the original Hippie" after he and his wife lived on the Polynesian island of Fatu-Hiva for a year in 1937, with little more than a knife and a metal pot to survive with. His discovery there of a statue of the bearded "Kon-Tiki" god led him to build a balsa-wood raft and float across the Pacific Ocean in 1947, to prove that ancient people from Peru could have settled Polynesia. Thor, who served in the Norwegian Military during WWII, could also be called one of the first peace activists and went on to be a force for cleaning up the increasing pollution in the oceans of the world. His enduring message to the public was, "Question Authority" a precept he affirmed by proving the scientific community wrong in the history of Pacific Migration. Throughout his life he lived by his "hippie ideals" and he was way ahead of his time, as an example of a free thinking human being.

Some of the hippie "peaceniks" became draft dodgers of the Vietnam War, during the late 60's. They had to move to Canada, Europe, or run for as long as it took to get out of the draft, or to be jailed as a political prisoner in such movements as the Weathermen. The anger at President Nixon for not ending the Vietnam War was intense and when Watergate happened and the war finally ended in 1975; the hippies were vindicated. Yet for many it was way too late. They had dropped out and tuned in to the new "back-to-the-land" movement. They saw the direction that America was taking and wanted a different life. The hippies were those who had gone through the Draft and the Vietnam War, the Civil Rights Movement, the Women's Liberation movement, the anti-nuclear movement and had paid the price for the so-called "drug-war" in America.

The Peace movement in the early 70's was a very powerful factor in bringing people together. Their beliefs were expressed as well as absorbed through the medium of modern rock music, such as the Beatles, Rolling Stones, Crosby-Stills-Nash and Young, the Grateful Dead, Jefferson Airplane, Jimi Hendrix, Bob Dylan, Donovan, The Doors, Beach Boys, Eagles and many other counter-culture groups and artists. The many influences for the counter-culture are too long to list but it can be said that writers like Jack Kerouac, Gary Snyder, Ken Kesey, Abbie Hoffman and Baba Ram Dass inspired them. The Woodstock generation was definitely a huge movement of people finding expression and liberation by traveling to protests, concerts, communes, hot springs, nudist colonies, be-ins, Rainbow festivals, and a variety of foreign destinations where the hip would gather.

One of the most popular destinations was the Haight-Ashbury district of San Francisco, where it seemed the youth were intent on partying their lives away and experimenting with drugs. People from all over the USA were gathering on the west coast, mainly California, and becoming part of the new hippie movement. Two of those early hippies were Mark K. and Romain C. who were high school buddies from New Orleans who had come to San Francisco. After meeting up they got part time jobs repairing old Victorian houses. Mark said, "It started getting kind of weird there. Thousands of displaced young people were arriving, very clueless about everything and hard drugs started showing up. We kind of knew we wanted to be in the country anyway so we fixed up an old truck and started exploring the west coast. We were camping out when we ran into somebody who said there's this place called Takilma and it's got a great swimming hole. So we went to check it out in July of 1970 and never left."

At this point, in the early 70's many people started to think of moving out of the cities and living closer to nature. This happened as people grew tired of the crowds and the police backlash that was triggered by student protests. One woman said, "We felt like we had to grab our babies and run to the country." Hippies, being romantics at heart, wanted an idealistic life where people lived in harmony with the natural cycles and planted organic gardens. Many had to sell everything and start from scratch.

Whole busloads and caravans of hippies had taken off from Berkeley in the late 70's to become farmers. Led by Stephen Gaskin, they drove to Tennessee, bought some farmland and 480 "charismatic leaders" began a grand experiment in living. Their example on "The Farm," inspired many thereafter.

Another place some of the hippies met was at a rock festival in Sandy, put on by the State of Oregon, in August of 1970. Governor McCall was worried about massive anti-war protests happening on the streets of Portland, during the week of the American Legion Convention, so he put out orders not to ticket young people, and to hand out flyers directing them to a free outdoor rock concert in McGuyver Park, calling it "The Vortex." Thousands of young long-haired hippies arrived and started setting up a festival. It happened spontaneously, that the people built an outdoor stage and organized the festival grounds. A steam bath was built in a tent, next to a hot mud bath. Then the naked people from the sauna would swim in the river. Many of the local businesses donated materials and the installation of a temporary kitchen. There was widespread drug use, and a barrel of wine in front of the stage, was said to spiked with LSD. But the police and the National Guard were on orders not to interfere. No one seemed to be in control, even though no real problems arose from all those people "in a hippie zoo."

A group calling itself "The Family" did much of the volunteer labor and manned the medical booth. Governor McCall's assistants monitored the festival, and the streets of Portland from a motel room and commented that they had achieved their objective; very little protesting went on. They later said, "We accomplished our goals, we channeled potential violence." Some of the hippies responded to allegations that they had sold out the anti-war movement, by saying what happened at the Vortex was in and of itself a form of non-violent protest. It was the only state sponsored rock concert in US history and was like a sort of Woodstock west, where mass nudity was experienced and a spiritual bond was created.

After the festival ended Gov. McCall came down to visit and toured the park. What happened was a "counter-culture collaboration with the State's highest official", as the Governor held hands and chanted OM with a group of hippies. It must have made a big impression because within a few years many initiatives were passed like Land Use Planning, the Beach Bill and the Bottle Bill which put Oregon in the lead on environmental issues. One of the earliest residents of Takilma, Robert H. said, "Lots of us who were there, ended up in Takilma later."

A party at the Takilma "Love House."
Photo by Robert Hirning

Boogie, Doug, Fuzzy and others at the old
"Love House." Photo by Robert Hirning

PART 4

The first Hippies arrive

Takilma in the early days was a mixture of old timers and hippies, but slowly the old timers sold their places and got away from a lifestyle they perhaps didn't care for anymore. Times had changed and the tables were turning. One man's trash can be another man's treasure, so Takilma was just that bit of gold dust to glimmer in the eyes of the new age hippies. It had been raped and pillaged, burned and degraded, but still the land lived on and welcomed a new wave of "green" people. Perhaps it can be said that the Indian Spirit reclaimed the land.

Here then, are a few of the voices of Takilma; certainly only a small slice of the whole pie, but definitely some people who have given a great deal to the quality of life, now enjoyed in Takilma. I mentioned the general reasons that a population of hippies found themselves living in Takilma, Oregon, but now I'd like to dig deeper into some of the stories about how people moved to Takilma and what made them stay.

One of the first "hippies" to move to Takilma was Delbert K., who came from Southern California in 1968 to the tiny, rural, unincorporated town of Takilma, because the land was cheap, remote, wild, un-improved, lawless, and largely un-inhabited. Delbert left behind a struggling business in Southern California and brought his family north, after receiving some letters from a friend in Oregon who worked at the old Takilma Store, describing a place "like paradise".

Upon first arrival in 1968, Helen had just given birth to her third child and they lived in a 3 room shack, in downtown Takilma until it got to be too small for their growing family. After returning to LA that winter they couldn't find another place to live and decided to come back to Takilma, determined to make it work. After trying to live on a commune known as the "Fanatic Family" on Dick George Rd., they finally settled into the little red house on Takilma Rd. In the years that followed many people came in search of their dreams and Delbert and Helen took them in or told them where to go to find shelter and food, usually at the crash pads in what was known as "The Riverbed."

One day Delbert's friend was hitchhiking out for a visit and was picked up a guy by the name of Jimbo who wanted to buy some pot. He told him, "If you give me a ride out to Takilma, I'm sure I can find you some." So as Delbert recalled, "Jimbo, after camping out down by the river at Papa Joe's, really took a liking to the place and stayed on and sold his pick up truck and changed the whole direction of his life. The next winter Jimbo was staying up at the Riverbed. There was a Deputy at the time named Medkiff, who really hated the hippies. He showed up at the Riverbed with a Health Officer and Jimbo cold-cocked the deputy with a gun and ran off into the bushes. So the Sheriff's Dept. rounded up hundreds of people and deputized them. They closed off Four Corners and for several days they went through everybody's house in Takilma. Jimbo, who had been watching in horror from the bushes where he was hidden, realized what he had done to his friends, and finally turned himself in. Well, for some strange reason they refused to arrest him. It sounded far-fetched to me at the time, but years later I found out it was true." Delbert continued his story, "That event really caught the eye of the press and the American Civil Liberties Union organized a debate in Medford, in which 3 or 4 hippies came to debate the Sheriff and the District Attorney. One of those hippies was me and it was one of the first televised meetings. At one point I stood up and said, 'Doesn't the Sheriff's Dept. have anything better to do than to hassle people about the relatively innocuous habit of smoking weed?' And the DA on the panel, a guy named Burroughs, stood up and said, 'Innocuous is it? But it's against the Law!!!' For years afterwards, people would stop me and say, 'Didn't I see you on TV?' or 'You made the DA look like a fool.' Later on that DA, became one of my friends."

So after all that drama, Delbert bought himself a chainsaw and decided to just go cut firewood. At first he gave much of it away to local friends and neighbors who needed it, and who often helped him do the work. Later he sold the firewood for $18 per cord. From those humble beginnings, he was able to eventually buy two horses and start a small horse-logging business to provide poles and lumber for residents to build with. "I didn't know anything about building, but somehow I decided we needed a house and just started building us a log cabin. We got this land in exchange for selling the lots on the neighbors 250 acres, which had just been split up."

Mark K. and Romain C. heard about some land across the river which "nobody owned." To get there you had to wade across the river and then walk a mile through the woods. They and a group of friends, including Patrick F. and Allen W. started to camp there. Mark said, "It was paradise. During that summer twenty other people showed up, and it was fantastic, and when the weather got cold in the fall we decided hey, let's stay. So we bought a salvage house for twenty bucks down in Rio Del California, tore it down and brought all that redwood lumber up here. We built five little shacks up there. Fifteen of us spent the winter."

"By the next spring word kind of got out; Takilma's really neat and lots of people were showing up, really neat people; lots of beautiful women and beautiful men. Beth showed up pretty early that summer," said Mark about his future partner. One visitor by the name of Paul McGill, unbeknownst to Mark and the others was actually the owner of the property, but didn't say anything. By the end of that summer, another 60-70 people showed up and there were camp fires everywhere. Things had gotten out of hand. People were building bonfires in August. Mark recalled the time there was a real serious fire, "Somebody was smoking and started a fire of about an acre up on the hillside. So the Forest Service sent tanker bombers out. The word got out and suddenly about 50 naked hippies ran up from the swimming hole and started to help. They called it the "Bare-Bottom Burn" after that. So we got the fire under control but meanwhile they sent an air tanker to spread fire retardant. They herded us over to one side but they bombed the hippies instead of the fire and all these naked hippies were all red and smoky, but the fire was finally out."

Mark continued with his story, "So the Forest Service told the landowner about it, and he came back a couple weeks later. He came to the garden and he said, 'This is crazy, you gotta leave. I don't mind a few people but this is too much.' So we said 'You should give us the land.' And he laughed but he said he would sell it to us. We said, 'But we don't have any money,' yet he said he would give us terms. He gave us a year to get the down payment. Right then it started coalescing. The people that wanted to live there and take care of the land got serious about raising the money to buy the land. That sort of weeded out the less serious people, who just wanted to have fun. It was a lot of hard work." So that was the beginning of the Meadows Commune.

Mark with a core group of hippies started having meetings and developing plans. Mark said, "We wanted to see what we could do with appropriate technology. We weren't sure but we could see where the world was heading and we wanted to get away from mainstream culture." As Mark explained, "It seemed like the world was going crazy. My friends were coming home either insane or in a box from Vietnam. So we were starting over with a new culture.

We thought we could do better. So we started out without anything. We literally didn't buy toilet paper for ten years; we hardly saw a movie or listened to music (other than the music we played ourselves) for ten years. We saved every cent to pay for the land. It was kind of an isolated world."

Many of the new residents heard about Takilma from word of mouth. Sheila heard about it from a friend, and came up in 1972. Sheila remembered, "I had two young children, and it was the whole movement of getting back-to-the-land, growing organic food and living a lifestyle that provided so much. Five families bought 20 acres together and we lived communally. We all had our own little cabins, but we shared a main kitchen and gardened together. It was a wonderful way to raise your children. It was very healthy."

Delbert and Sitting Dog—Photo by Jim Shames

The Takilma Store in 1972—Photo of
oil painting, by Alan Laurie

PART 5

Why Did They Come?

D red Mikal came to Takilma with his young wife Kathy to have their first child. Tahiti was born with the help of the "Birthmobile" in a small cabin on Hope Mountain given to them by Stanley and Fauna. Dred Mikal remembered, "They gave us this cabin and a horse came with it." After purchasing the "old boarding house" Dred Mikal went on to raise his family there and got by with a variety of forestry jobs and seasonal fruit picking jobs. He had to repair and renovate the place and is still in the process of restoring the building.

When asked what it was like back then, Dred Mikal remembered a place up the river called the "Seed Company" which consisted of a group of people living in what was known as the "Octagon" and who had radical ideas about fixing the earth. "All these dreadlocked characters were living there in their greenhouses." A sign above their door said, "Plant the fruits of paradise" and they followed this philosophy by suddenly appearing at people's houses and bringing everything needed to plant them a garden. "They never asked for anything, this was just their vision that we could all be feeding ourselves." Dred Mikal has been in Takilma for 36 years, raised his family and tried to attain a degree of self-sufficiency by growing his own food in his garden and greenhouse. He still has an old horse drawn cart and buggy in which he occasionally takes people out for a drive. He is an example of the pioneer spirit which is still alive in Takilma's hippie movement.

Other reasons the hippies came to Takilma were more nebulous, because there was just a general migration from south to north and from east to west, as young people hitchhiked all over the country, commune hopping and looking for great places to be. They came from the cities to find a better place in the country, where they could find refuge in the small neglected towns and homesteads dotting the west.

Back when Robert was living in Marin County, he heard a lot of rumors of this mythical place called Takilma, just over the border in Oregon where it was still really wild. As Robert recounts, "So one day on the beach in 1971 I met up with Rainbow Bob (so called because one eye was blue and the other brown) and we just started hitchhiking up the coast. It took us 3 days, (which it seems we spent more of our time drinking wine on the side of the road) but we finally found Takilma and spent our first night across the river from the Mirage Garage. Charlie Two Shoes was there to welcome us and it was really *different*." It was quite a happening back then and there were up to 30 people camping at different communes, and building more rough and unusual shelters to live in. Robert recalled, "On my first day I was spending some time up at Rowdy Ridge, when I saw six guys carrying a wood stove up the river, laughing and talking as they went. I just looked at them and thought; this is so wild and crazy! Takilma was a place where you could find yourself in a circle with lots of crazy, wonderful people who all shared a positive, communal energy!" Soon, Robert was able to buy a piece of land on Takilma Road for the amazingly low price of $2,500. It had a small cabin, and was named the Funky Egg Company, after the 70 odd chickens that Robert had trucked up from California.

Early in 1973, there were no phones and little transportation so Ranger John Hoffman called a meeting, where he hand-picked a crew from the hippies and others that showed up for work. Robert, Otto, Randall, Ron T., Alan K. and up to 40 others found employment on the fire crew with the Forest Service. "That summer we were fighting fires all over and earning $3 per hour. Suddenly there was work", said Robert.

The next winter Ranger Hoffman again hand-picked a crew of 25 of the strongest hippies to do winter tree planting, a job which many Americans found too physically challenging. After proving their competence in the harsh conditions they banded together and formed a small company called "Green Side Up." They got a contract with the Forest Service to plant trees for $8.00 per hour. Eventually, after some financial backing from friends, they landed a $100,000 contract and were able to keep people working locally on reforestation sites around the Illinois Valley. Some of these places were the most inaccessible and rugged locations to be found and workers often had to climb steep hillsides. People's skills and endurance were sorely tested.

Randall was one of the earliest tree planters with Green Side Up and recalls "I already had a background trimming trees with the Parks Dept., so then they taught me how to rope climb to the top of the trees. I attended Green Side Up meetings and got on a list. From then on I worked at planting trees for the reforestation program, and we worked at fencing, planting, tagging and mapping. By the time we were done those trees were worth about 200 bucks each! Each tree was two years old and species were matched up to a unit on an elevation basis. Everybody has heard of super trees. I was in the program of "cone heads", only eight of us who would document and pick all the cones. I have worked in forestry for 25 years, from Gold Beach to Lakeview."

Randall remarked, "I'm surprised that I was able to live and work here for so many years on such low wages, but I've always lived well and feel really blessed. Our weather is better than ¾'s of the world." Randall enjoys a musical career these days as a guitar and dobro player in a band called "The Occasional Two-Timing Double-Crossers." He says, "We're kinda rowdy and radical." He adds wryly, "I just almost cut my index finger off. Now I have to use my other fingers more to play the guitar." This kind of independent, hard working spirit is an example of the never-give-up attitude of the hippies.

Shelley H. plants trees in the Chetco
Basin. Photo by Robert Hirning

Kerry W. planting trees with Green Side
Up. Photo by Robert Hirning

Robert H. at the Funky Egg Co. Photo by Robert Hirning

PART 6

The Old Cook Ranch

Doug and Alyce K. of Doo-Dah, spoke of how they came to Takilma. "My brother John and his wife Della had just moved here, a few months prior, with a group of their friends from Santa Barbara, and so we came up just to visit them", recalled Alyce, "It was a time in our lives when we were looking for what was next." "And awhile became 40 years," chuckled Doug with a twinkle in his eyes." Alyce added, "The group from Santa Barbara had planned and talked about the Back to the Earth movement, but no that really wasn't our motivation at the time. But, when we got here, yeah, then it definitely fit all of our beliefs and what we wanted to do at that point. It just kind of evolved that way."

Doug had graduated with a Master's Degree from the Rhode Island School of Design, and Alyce was teaching. As Doug recalled, "Lou and Delia found this 40 acres and we just happened in on our grand tour. We rented the Cook ranch house and lived in that for the first year, until we got our house built." Meanwhile they and their land partners were building a geodesic Dome on Doo Dah. This Dome was built from plans found in the Dome Book II, published by Whole Earth Catalog. It was a hippie dream which took many hands to build.

When more money was needed Doug worked on the Green Side Up crew and some of the women also wanted the jobs. Alyce along with Della, Shannon, Beth, Suedah, Rabbitt, Shelley and Jean P. were among the first women hired on to work planting trees in the early 70's. These women were pioneers of equality of the sexes and often were given some of the most challenging jobs, to test their resolve. Joya joined the crew in 1981. The much needed wages provided, in Joya's case, a car and a woodstove; the essentials of life in the back-woods.

When that dried up, Alyce, who said, "I had experienced that I could find work teaching in most places," took a job as a substitute teacher at Evergreen Elementary. Doug, never comfortable with the label, "hippie", preferred that people use the term "long hair" instead, as he worked to integrate with the larger community. Doug reflected, "You need to wear several hats to survive. Having the Master's Degree, I was able to find a job teaching part-time at Rogue Community College in 1973. I also did a fair amount of wood crafts early on. In 1978, I finally started my house design drafting business and have been doing plans ever since."

The first residents of DooDah, had purchased the land as four consecutive parcels of the old Cook Ranch. As Doug recalled, "Bill F. was a local lawyer who bought the 200 acre Cook Ranch, sub-divided it into small parcels and really made a killing in the process." Doug added, "He often asked me to help him show the lots in exchange for a break on the rent for the Cook ranch house." Later Bill and Cathy D. purchased that house and others from Santa Barbara came up and bought neighboring parcels. Doug's brother Dave was able to buy some of those lots too.

The next spring the families of the DooDah commune, were building their own "bedroom" cabins on nearby hillsides, while still cooking meals in the Dome and living communally. Those were years of bonding and closeness between the four young families that shared the land and gardened and worked together. Said Alyce, "For all the years that I taught; I went to work and Doug was the house husband." She added, "There was a whole lot of male/female equity in the building of the DooDah Dome. Things were open to anyone who wanted to try it. The women also felt, that being liberated meant, hey if he's really good at it, and he's better trained at it, then let him do it!"

Doug's young family grew with the birth of two daughters and Alyce, along with Helen, Judith Ann and Jake M. were instrumental in starting the fledgling school in the Dome. Some friends came to help. Donalee said, "Pook and I went up there and told them, well you have enough kids up here already, so just start a school in the Dome. So we brought our kids up there every day and we all taught them together. That was the birth of the Dome School in 1975." The need for education and health care were needs that were shared by many of the women with young babies growing up. And there were a lot of babies being born. The growth of the fledgling Takilma People's Clinic was "started by a need to help people have their kids," as Doug recalled, "Necessity was the mother of invention." As Alyce recalled, "A lot of the people that came in the 70's were educated in several skills, they were really do-ers and they had directions and desires. Three of the original teachers at the Dome School were certified teachers, and wanted to be of service." To sum it all up, Doug concluded, "It was really unique here, and organizing gave us clout. From the beginning we formed unusual alliances with the people around here."

Rachel heard about Takilma from where she was staying on the Oregon coast. "We were really looking for our own space among other people. We heard this was a very interesting area, and we also heard that in Grants Pass the hippies and the cowboys were shooting each other. So we said, oh well, we're going to the coast; at least we'll be safe there!" She had a young son, Bear and wanted the best possible education for him. After visiting she realized how much Takilma offered; "Having neighbors, and the county road, having the Wonder Dome for supplies, and having the Takilma Clinic," were the reasons she listed for her decision to stay. The new little Dome School allowed her to be closely involved in her son's education and as a result she found many kindred souls. She also found a lot for sale, from the old Cook Ranch and bought it for a quite reasonable fee. She had found a bit of paradise by the river, where she could walk to the Dome School. As Rachel remembers the way she got by in the early days, "Learning more about gardening and focusing so we could produce food and getting trained for a career that I could get income out of. We were all thinking about self-sufficiency. We have always cared passionately about our children. A lot of us, as our children entered the school system felt that the culture just demands that they have nice shoes and stuff. Somewhere along the line I developed an interest in massage therapy and started classes at Rogue Community College." Rachel, now the owner of her own massage business thinks that "Takilma offers just a vibrant, interesting community that's in the mix that's the Illinois Valley."

People were starting to trickle in from around the country, attracted by friends and acquaintances who recommended the sleepy little forested village of eccentric, young people. Rachel wondered what percentage of people in Takilma, were really college-educated. She recalled, "There was a big mix. Kids were coming up from LA, and dropping out of high school." Rachel remembers how things were back then, she summarized her feelings with, "There was just a lot of wanting to let go of everything, and then you have to pick up the pieces and find out what really matters. People of similar backgrounds fell together. I remember visiting the Meadows when Bear was little and they were all carrying water and sawing wood with bow-saws."

Mark from the Meadows explained that, "We didn't come across the river that much back then, because we didn't have a bridge. Occasionally we did wade across to spend time with the larger community. We spent a lot of time cutting firewood by hand for everybody and digging the garden. That was the big thing, we didn't have a rototiller so we would line out across the garden with shovels and dig up an acre and a half of land. It was gratifying to know you could do it, if you had to, but it ends up you didn't do much else."

Takilma work crew for the Community
Building-Photo by Jim Shames

The Old DooDah Dome-Photo by Robert Hirning

Alyce teaching in the old Dome School-
Photo by Jim Shames

PART 7

The Takilma Forge and Stories from Jim

People like Jim R. were coming from college degrees, professional lives, and trading them in for humble digs in Takilma. Jim was a producer of classical records who, bored of his job, took off for Pennsylvania to learn blacksmithing. That summer of 1974 he headed west, and stumbled on the town of Takilma after driving all the way through to Sun Star at night, in hopes of finding his friends. The mythical place, Sun Star was akin to a Shangri-la for hippies and had attracted many people with tales of its remote beauty. Jim lived at Sun Star until 1978.

The next few years were times of big changes, as hippies were slowly assimilated into the Illinois Valley. Jim recalled one event which really affected how people perceived the police. "John Boy and his friend were riding their motorcycle on 199 near O'Brien one day, when a carload of Orange County deputies on their way to a convention ran them off the road. Well, they went back to the pay phone in O'Brien and called the Sheriff with their report and gave a description and even a license number. Well, sure enough, those guys were arrested on their way back to Grants Pass and they said, 'but they're just some hippies!!' to which the Sheriff replied, 'Oh yeah, well you can do whatever you want to your hippies, but these are OUR hippies and you're not gonna hurt em!!!" It seemed that hippies were finding some unexpected allies.

During those early years Jim met Delbert who was keeping his mules up in the Sun Star barn. Soon they traded their skills and Jim was shoeing horses for Delbert. Jim recalls his first job in Takilma. "Yusef wanted a bracket made for his wooden butcher block table, and he wanted to trade me some elk hides for it. I later made my bellows out of those hides." Soon Sun Star became "like a three ring circus", and he was invited to come to T.a.'s land and start a commune there. "The very next day, I was building the shop at T.a.'s (which is still there) and everything I owned was moved there. I also helped build another little log cabin there," said Jim. Soon Jim acquired an apprentice; Michael L. from Magic Forest Farm. He found out about some land for sale downtown. Jim recalled, "Michael looked up the number, dialed it and handed the phone to me. Mr. Putlitz owned a prime spot, but couldn't pass the perk test for a septic system, so he sold it to me for what he paid. I bought it the next day, in 1981." Jim continued, "I had been shoeing horses for Delbert for 5 or 6 years and one day, when he heard that I bought this, he came to me, to his credit, and said, would you trade for framing and roofing a building here? I said, you bet!! The very next day he had a crew over here to start." Eventually Jim, "made trip after trip in my old Chevy pick-up, to get all those boards with the bark edges from his portable sawmill. The price was right!"

Once the place was built, his rustic, blacksmithing shop made wagon wheels, hinges, fireplace tools, kitchen tools and implements with embellishments of artistic ironwork. Ironically Jim, who lived a life without luxuries in a small cabin added to the back of his shop, still read by candlelight and enjoyed his voluntary simplicity. He was a respected craftsman yet also a talented musician, who played beautiful baroque classical music on the flute, oboe and recorder. Jim recalls the earliest beginnings of his Jefferson Baroque Orchestra. "I was visiting friends the first winter in Sun Star, who'd come up from Santa Barbara and I knew that they were both musicians. So I found some of my old sheet music and took it to Steve and Sher's cabin and asked them if they'd like to play, and they said sure. So I taught them this music called "Oh My Heart; a Little Love Song" by Henry VIII. In 15 minutes we were singing it as if we'd been singing it all our lives. So within a year we had added Suedah and we had a soprano. Soon we had four of us singing with a repertoire of 40 songs we could sing by heart. So in 1976 we went as a group to the Country Faire and walked right through the gates, singing and in costume and everybody just assumed we belonged. We didn't buy food the whole three days! Later I started going as a blacksmith." When asked why he chose to play Baroque music, Jim intoned, "Order; it's logical, temperate, symmetrical, and at the same time there is an element of freedom and improvisation in it" as he showed me his beautiful hand-built harpsichord.

No stranger to hard work, Jim was one of the earliest volunteers at the new Takilma Fire Station, built in the early 80's. When asked how it was that the station got built, Jim recounted the strange events leading up to that. "There was a time when the Sheriff's Department was doing a lot of busts for marijuana. This particular year, they had started using a lot of reserve deputies, who were basically volunteers who had no discipline whatsoever, and would just go in and tear a place apart" said Jim. So, "When the word got out that a couple carloads of deputies had gone up Duvall's Road to bust Dan K., about 200 very angry hippies blockaded the road, so they couldn't get out. They thought they were doomed, and they called for help. About two hours later, (it took awhile to marshal all their resources and call for the Fire Dept) so after this long motorcade passed to go up there, the obstacles were put back on the road. It then took them another two to three hours to get out of town. I remember there were four or five deputies, with shotguns at port arms, facing this angry crowd, walking backwards and just scared to death. One of the hippies walked up to one of these scared deputies and points a finger at him and said, 'I smoked dope with you!' And someone else said, 'Yeah, immature bud', because everybody knew that the stuff they confiscated, well very little of it ended up as evidence."

Jim continued his story, "A week later they did the same thing again and again. The Sheriff's Department in those raids spent two years of budget and overtime, because it cost so much. Meanwhile Chief Yanase, was just furious at getting involved in this. The very next day he was at the Clinic apologizing and they got to talking about how the Fire Department could better serve Takilma. So the Chief mentioned E. Dittman, a gentleman who had a place right on the SW corner of Four Corners. He had a little triangle of property that he was willing to give to the Fire Department and after talking to Dr. Jim and the people at the Clinic, he decided to accept that offer and build his station there. Chief Yanase refuted the Sheriff's actions and placed himself entirely on the side of our community. So that was how the station got built, and when the rigs arrived there were quite a group of people who were volunteers from Takilma." From that time on, until the Fire of '87 Jim was a volunteer fire-fighter, and served as Captain for two years.

Jim R. at the Takilma Forge-Photo courtesy of Jim Rich

Jim R. blacksmithing at the Oregon Country
Faire. Photo courtesy of Jim Rich

PART 8

The Takilma People's Clinic

D r. Jim S. accepted an offer to be sent down to Takilma from Portland in 1973 after a severe Hepatitis A outbreak which caused a few desperate hippies to seek help from the Josephine County Health Department. Robert H. said, "I was exposed to Hepatitis A and it was really bad so I went down to the Health Dept. and they looked at me with loathing, and wouldn't give me a gamma globulin shot." When the authorities up north got word of this outbreak they sent Dr. Jim down fresh from a medical degree at the University of Wisconsin. Robert added, "That Hepatitis A outbreak was huge in Takilma, really important, because after that was when things finally started to improve."

Dr. Jim invited a newly released medic from the Green Berets, Michael G., to join him in healing the people. Michael said, "He asked me come down with him and help set up a clinic."

After finding a community of like-minded people, Dr. Jim fell in love with Heidi P. and found himself invited to live at the Magic Forest Farm. He was starting out on a career as a country doctor. Before long the community, led by Delbert donated their time and materials to build Dr. Jim and his young family a log cabin. Dr. Jim was very much appreciated because there was such a severe need for medical care and his simple and respectful ways as a country doctor endeared him to many. As Helen remarked, "I've always thought he was just a cut above the ordinary person because of the dedication he had for this community and the entire Illinois Valley. He was just amazing!" The small, rural clinic started in an old house on Takilma Rd. but soon moved to the Takilma Community Association building on the hill in 1975.

Sue D. from DooDah, who had some childbirth instruction from nursing school, was one of the first people to sign on at the new Takilma People's Clinic where the care was literally free. (Even though some paid with eggs, garden produce, a cow and even a vial of gold dust once.) She helped come up with the idea of a "Birthmobile" so they could attend the many home births that were happening. She and Dr. Jim had gone up north for training at the Oregon Health Sciences to handle deliveries and emergencies. A panel truck was outfitted for anything the attendants and the birthing parents would need, including emergency equipment. She and several more people, including Joya F. and Lisa K. got additional training as midwifes. At countless home births, Dr. Jim would come to assist the midwives when needed and provided the skills and services of having a trained doctor present. One of Dr. Jim's most famous quotes about that time was, "We were all motivated by all the right reasons. We took a lot of chances. We did what we had to do. It was my job to keep everyone safe."

Sue recounts that, "Dr. Jim was dedicated to teaching everyone what he knew. In those days we were innocent and naïve because that was before people even heard of medical malpractice. The Clinic was such a needed service, in such a good community, that it was fun to go there." Of the roughly 2,000 births that Sue attended, they had a perfect safety record, a remarkable accomplishment. She said, "We were able to screen out high-risk women and later we even served as an ambulance to take patients in." Sue admits to needing the services of the "Birthmobile" herself with the delivery of her second child. She remembered that, "It was a good thing because Teva was born in the middle of a cold winter night, and the Birthmobile was there in case I needed to go to the hospital." Randall remembers being rescued by the Birthmobile, when Dr. Jim, Sue and Lisa came to his son's birth. He said, "That's another special thing about Takilma. I relied on them. I still don't really trust anyone outside of Takilma."

Joya, one of the apprentice midwives, came to Takilma after she completed Nursing School in Ashland to be part of the birthing team. She started out volunteering for six months then received a small stipend of $50 per month until it slowly increased. The Takilma midwives helped establish protocols for safe midwifery practice for the Oregon Midwifery Council and facilitated educational opportunities for midwives around the state. The midwives also received training in family planning services. Of course she was doing much more than home births, she was a nurse for many of her patients and their family's medical needs. Joya recalls, "I came here to be an apprentice midwife. Getting called to births was quite a trick for me where I live, because back in those early days we didn't have a footbridge, and when the water was high I'd have to walk out through the back of the gulch. It was more than a mile to hike out to get to the road. Things were really primitive here for quite awhile. For me to be notified about a pending birth, either a call would come to a neighbor, someone would come to get me on horseback, or someone would yell across the river for me, and there were a few times when it was just pure intuition and I would wake up in the middle of the night and I could just sense that someone was in labor. I'd pack up my baby and my bag and hike out, and the few times that happened, I was right." Later a birth room was outfitted at the Clinic and babies were born there when possible. The last births at the Clinic were in 1987 right after the Longwood Fire.

The Clinic and the Dome School were started by the more or less college educated hippies, to meet the needs of their growing community. Jake M. came as a guest of his girlfriend Judith Ann, who was working down in the Bay area at the Rivendell School. As he recalls, "I had heard all these things about the Farm. We knew that there were families up there at the Farm and DooDah that were wanting to have a community school and we were teaching at an alternative school. We came in the middle of February and I fell in love with the Farm." Jake and Judith Ann finally moved in to the Farm in 1975 and found a refuge in nature. "The orchards and garden were planted in 1968 by the first residents and we could just plug in. Everyone was involved in the Clinic or the School. There were lots of potlucks." Jake recalled that "The first night I set foot in Takilma, the store was still smoking, it had just burned down and there wasn't much of a town." So the small commune became a hard-working group of dedicated people who were creating the foundation of a town themselves. Jake recalled that "The birthmobile came to Molly's birth," in the old days. Soon he and Judith Ann started helping build the new Takilma Community Building, also the future home of the Dome School. It was a very busy time.

Other challenges back in the 70's were living without adequate services like flush toilets and showers. Keeping clean and washing clothes was difficult, since trips to the laundromat were expensive. It was during the early 70's that a bath house was built at the "Barn" which allowed residents to come to bathe for free and use a shower, sauna and hot tub. Robert, with a dedicated interest in public health recalls how his interest in plumbing started. It was due to his college degree in Archaeology that he felt an unusual enjoyment of digging up ditches for pipes. He realized how much people needed to get clean, so he and a group of hippies, designed a facility and started work. Looking back now Robert said, "I didn't know I wanted to be a plumber until I started putting pipes together." The entire project took 8 months to complete and cost $600. Most of the fixtures were recycled from a house-wrecking job in Grants Pass. The Bath House finally opened right before Christmas, 1972.

Sheila started out volunteering at the new Takilma Clinic. She remembers that, "I really loved the sense of community, and I really believed in the mission, which was to serve people with health care." Sheila worked as the Clinic's receptionist and office manager for 33 years. Sheila said that, "Some people went on to other jobs, but for me it was ideal. I had two children and the Clinic had child care, so it worked for me. It was very educational for me." When asked what it was like to work with Dr. Jim, she said, "It was wonderful, wonderful! He is a very kind and knowledgeable man, who was in a teaching role constantly. All the people who worked at the Clinic were really nice. The dedication was heart moving."

Jonny was a genius with a PhD Degree from MIT, who came up from Berkeley with a group of young hippie idealists to found a commune known as Talsalsan. His particular skills, fresh from a successful career as a NASA research scientist, would become very important to the formation of several Takilma organizations. Besides his expertise in computers, ham radios and legal matters, Jonny could play the trombone.

In 1973, the Takilma Community Association was created, to help with community administrative support and advocacy. Jonny K., Joe P. and Elaine S. drew up the By-Laws and legal papers for the small non-profit. As Doug recalled, "Jonny was such a brilliant mind, and he did know the legal jargon." As part of their stated mission of supporting community projects, they also were a holding company for open land in Takilma, to keep the valley free of development. People really valued the open space and the view of the Siskiyou Mountains. The land called the old Webb House, the Alcorn House next to it and the valley land known as the "ball field" were all purchased with community donations and are held by the small community organization to protect the land for future generations.

In 1975 the Clinic opened on TCA property, in the old Alcorn house which had been remodeled. Doug was in on the job and one day he was working with John Whiteside finishing up an addition to the front of the building, when 5 cop cars pulled up to cite the Clinic for building code violations. Doug said, "There was a big confrontation. They were overly aggressive in the beginning so that caused the revolt which led to an alliance between right and left thinking people." The group wrote a letter, which exposed the unfair rules, the lack of citizen advisory groups, and asked that the County ensure that the codes did not make it more difficult for rural people to build their own homes in Oregon. They insisted, "No inspection without representation!" This case in which Jonny K. and John W. were defendants spurred a complete review and overhaul of the building codes in Josephine County, leading the judge to dismiss the case. The notorious "Code for the Abatement of Dangerous Buildings" (initiated by the County in an attempt to run off the hippies) was also rescinded at that time by popular demand.

The Takilma People's Clinic opened for business and helped all comers regardless of ability to pay. It was expanding and involving community people, by having one person "On call" each night. They slept in the clinic at night answering calls and could get some credit for it too. The clinic was serving so many, because the entire Illinois Valley was medically underserved. It provided numerous jobs and training opportunities for anyone who desired it, and eventually started charging a sliding-scale for its services.

The Birthmobile and staff-Photo courtesy of Jim Shames

Dr. Jim and his family at home at the Farm-
Photo courtesy of Jim Shames

The Old Takilma Bath House-Photo by Robert Hirning

The Takilma People's Clinic volunteers in
1974. Photo courtesy of Jim Shames

PART 9

The Communes

It is important to note that it was during those early years that the beliefs and values of the hippies were envisioned, tested, expressed, developed, and refined in the form of a true "community." There were a great deal of ideas and once the people settled in to a comfortable living situation they started to work on different community projects. There was always a reverence for the natural forests and a feeling of stewardship for the land. People lived lightly on the land in small cabins dotting the landscape and many undertook building a home, if they were lucky enough to get in on some land. Contrary to public opinion, the hippies showed a surprising work ethic, and a passion to learn the arts of country living. Helen said, "We learned from some of the local people how to do things for survival every year. We found out they were just people like us and from there we got to know them. There was a free exchange of ideas." There were the workers; the ones who made things happen, and then there were the others who just wanted to party. Still people accepted, helped and supported each other with remarkably few problems. What is amazing is how they collaborated on projects and all the while still managed to have a rollicking good time.

Sherry Lou and Michael S. came to the community in 1970 and hung out across from the future Takilma Bible Church on land known as Rowdy Ridge. They also hung out at the Meadows until they bought some land near 4 corners and built a cabin. After two years they sold it and moved out on the Illinois River Road in Selma. They and another couple shared some land and lived a primitive existence in the remote area. As Sherry Lou explained it, "We were Horse people. Michael did everything. It was wonderful living out there. I was a very young Christian and I wanted to experience the presence of the Lord in my life. So one day, I walked out on a mountain. It was the most wonderful experience. I walked a trail that went to a waterfall and met with the Lord." Her love of nature and the beauty of the Kalmiopsis wilderness brought her the most exciting times of her life. Sherry Lou, who sewed hand-made velvet Navaho skirts on a treadle sewing machine, would become quite successful with selling her wares at the annual Oregon Country Faire.

One of the hallmarks of the Hippie movement was the communes and Takilma had many communes. Five main communes still exist today; Magic Forest Farm, the Meadows, DooDah, Cedar Gulch and Sun Star. Most of these communes have evolved into collective cooperatives of friends and neighbors. The success of the Takilma communes is an indicator of how stable and successful the entire community has become. People from these communes became the leaders of the community in many instances and helped to form organizations like the Takilma Community Association. Early commune residents were instrumental in starting the TCA, and have been volunteering for the Takilma Community Building, the Dome School and many of the other organizations for up to 40 years. They have been the ones to remain over the decades and do the work required.

In the early days the Meadows was purchased by a group of 25 hippies who raised the down payment, as told by Mark K. in his story about the early Meadows history and the fire in Scotch Gulch. Mark said that the Meadows land had long been abused: "Hydraulic mined, logged and grazed for over 100 years by the cattle from Duvall's Ranch, so it was not treated well and the garden soil was quite poor. It is now a lot better." Over the years many of the early people opted out due to the hard work and challenges of living off the grid and without road access. Now there is only a core group of a few families left. Mark recounts how they adapted to the remote lifestyle. He and his land mates were partners in developing alternative energy systems for the Meadows.

Mark said, "About ten years later, we started using our spare energy and money to construct water systems. We built a small hydro-electric system, with a bunch of home-made spoon like things which spun a small motorcycle generator and charged a car battery. We used that to light our house for four or five years. So we gradually got into technology that we felt was better. It's not like we were trying to secede from society, but we were just trying to figure out what worked." Some that worked were solar hydro-electricity, gravity-fed irrigation systems, solar hot water and wood-fired hot water to name a few.

Today the Meadows has their own hydro and solar energy systems, and enjoys full power off the grid. Mark chuckled, "It's gotten to the point now where it's more reliable than Takilma's power system." They have learned what works and adapted more and more technology to fit their needs. They also avoid the use of gas combustion engines with the use of electric golf carts to get around their land in recent years. Mark said, "Electric golf carts are like little electric mules. We use them to haul all of our firewood, to haul manure, produce and our supplies. We even use them for dragging logs to a small bandsaw mill used for lumbermaking. We do Lomakatsi type restoration forestry to thin the softwood out. We burn a lot of softwood."

Mark and Beth realized that tree planting and trail work was not going to last, so they were looking around for other ways to make a living. Mark remembers that, "We had always loved baskets and we read an article on how to make a basket out of Eastern black ash. So I found an Oregon ash tree and from that first tree we made a bunch of baskets and we sold out at the Oregon Country Faire that first year. So after much trial and error in figuring out how to find just the right tree, we gradually started making more and more baskets in a small workshop. That was the beginning of our business called *Splintworks*." One of the most popular basket designs was a distinctive backpack type basket, which many of the hippies used to carry their stuff around.

Mark talked about how the Meadows people became more involved with the community during the 80's. He said, "One thing we found out was there was a power in groups. With a group of folks with like minds you can do a lot. You can all start a Clinic together, you can all start a Green Side Up Co-op and build a school and community building together and take turns doing it. I think there's an amplification of energy that happens with groups of people. There's also problems; it's not always easy." Yet that led to the development of several Takilma organizations which paved the way for progress in the community.

Today the Meadows has become a beautiful place with their over 3 acres of organic gardens and orchards which are among the most successful in Takilma. Their homes rest gracefully in tune with the surrounding ecology and allow the residents to live in comfort and be extraordinarily self-sufficient. Mark said, "Now I appreciate having electricity and a bridge!"

Joya told me the story of how she came to live on land adjacent to the Meadows. "I first landed in a squatter cabin on BLM land in Allen Gulch, close to where I live now. The BLM kept threatening to burn down all our cabins, so I talked to the Krauss's about purchasing this land, but at the time they said no way. But gratefully enough, a few years later they did contact us. In the meantime I had purchased a small lot from Patrick M. which was adjacent to the Krauss's land. It was the only place with electricity, a telephone, and an indoor bathtub, so the Meadows people would come down to use them."

Soon Joya met Bill a friend who often came to the Illinois Valley to visit his friend Lisa K. and her family who were living at Trooper Tom's cabin. Bill was a botanist and wildlife biologist. After successfully tutoring Joya in algebra, Bill decided to follow her and Lisa down to LA for a few months where they would be training at the Harbor/UCLA Women's Health Care Nurse Practitioner Program. Joya recalls, "Bill decided he loved me so much that he wanted us to live together. Our relationship really deepened while we were in LA, and those were wonderful, sweet months, the three of us sharing a home together."

When they returned, Bill moved in with Joya on the East Fork and the next summer Rough and Ready logged the land that they eventually purchased. Joya said, "It was a really painful summer watching the forest that we loved come down tree by tree. But after they logged it they approached us with an offer and we were able to buy it for $1,000 per acre, by partnering with the Meadows people who wanted access to a good site for the new foot bridge." In the early 80's a giant tree with a rootball came down and tangled up the original bridge. It has since been replaced by both Joya and Bill and the Meadows families with a metal foot bridge, of much sturdier design. Joya recalls, "Those were amazing days of people searching for new ways of living and ways to connect and ways to be gentler with the land and gentler with each other." Joya remembers those early days, "I fell in love with the land and the river. I've set my roots down deeply. Just the beauty of the land, the place, it all sustains my body and my spirit."

Laurie P. one of the founders of Cedar Gulch tells a brief story of its beginnings, "Cedar Gulch was a homestead around 1929, owned by the Ed Michel's family. In the 60's, Cedar Gulch was sold to Ed Atkins, the pharmacist of Cave Junction who then sold it to Beaver and his wife." In 1971, Kerry H., Chris K. and Dan S. purchased the 80 acres known as Cedar Gulch. Within a couple years, Chris moved on and Penny and Laurie P. joined Kerry and Dan living at the 'gulch'. Laurie recalls her early years, "At that time there was only the original homestead house which became the communal house. We heated and cooked on a wood stove and had kerosene lamps for light. Many people came and went over the next 20 years. More individual homes were built, electricity was installed but we still maintained our Cedar Gulch Family. The garden continued to be our place of coming together during those years. Being as the gulch is at the end of the road, bordered by the Forest Service and BLM land, we relied on each other for help and support."

The Cedar Gulch commune was a fertile breeding ground for new creative pursuits. The first issue of the Takilma Common Ground newsletter was produced there. Laurie explained, "Common Ground began with the desire to create a local, community paper. The first few years, Common Ground was typed on one of the first apple computers and printed on a dot matrix printer at Cedar Gulch. Jill B. and Cathy H. would draw right on the original copies to be taken to be photo copied. They were true works of love. Lots of laughter and free flowing creativity went into publishing those papers."

Laurie who raised her two sons at Cedar Gulch, also had a great deal of involvement with the creation of the Dome School. She remembers how, "the Dome School helped all of our children become the wonderful beings they are today; giving them love, self-esteem, letting them be who they are and feel good about themselves."

Another commune resident who also had a great deal to do with the development of the Dome School, tells about how she found Takilma.

Kathcrinc R. was one of the earliest residents of the Sun Star commune. She remembers coming up to Oregon for a visit when she was only nineteen. "I was just a teenager and I had heard about Takilma from some of my older peers, and you know it was the "back-to-the-land movement" going on. So we came up here in the fall on Labor Day, and we asked about Takilma and a hippie picked up a hippie! So she was going out to Takilma and she took us, swimming. So later, we decided to keep on going looking for a place to camp, but we didn't see a thing. It looked like we were in the middle of the wilderness. We set up camp, and I guess we got kinda noisy, when out of the forest walks this lady; real, nice lady. So we were asking her if she knew of anyplace to caretake, when she said, 'You can caretake my house, I'm going back to Chicago in a couple weeks!' So it just fell into place for me. I felt like a pioneer for real, because it was basically a goat shed that we were caretaking. In those days a lot of people were living like that. So we made it through the first winter, and boy was that rough. I wrote a lot of poetry, drew a lot of pictures, had a lot of philosophical discussions, you know it was beautiful.

I have a Journal that I wrote through that winter and it was a good time of contemplation. So that's how I came here, and ended up buying into Sun Star. It was a goal that I had, to be a part of a community, so I was delighted that Sun Star sold shares. It was really affordable; of course it was a real primitive piece of land on the side of a mountain, and there was nothing on it, and no roads to it. But I didn't care; I was just comfortable with it. I lived in a tipi; the Rainbow Gathering was coming by here near Roseburg, so for me it was my Summer of Love, it was a really magical summer. The Grateful Dead were playing, Santana was playing in Eugene and the Country Faire was happening, and it was wonderful, everyone was coming through."

Katherine continued, "But by the end of the summer, I knew I was not prepared. So that's when I went to Hawaii for a year. I worked over there as a baker and got some skills and adventure. Then I moved back to the Bay area, and went to college in Oakland. I also worked and saved up money. I saved enough to have a little cabin built on the side of the mountain."

Katherine, was traveling between work in the Bay Area, and her place in Takilma. The next year she experienced logging next to her land. This was her first awareness of environmental issues in the Siskiyou National Forest. She recalls the time, "They clear cut right next to my land. There was a beautiful old growth forest right next to my land; big, big trees. Nobody knew what to do back then. We were shocked and wounded and our land was compromised. People were also starting to organize against the spraying of aerial defoliants. So everybody was doing that. There were conflicts and it was scary, but who was going to let them spray these defoliants they used in Vietnam? So that really impacted me."

Later after returning to the Bay Area to further her education and earn more money, she fell in with the Earth First group at a meeting at the University. Katherine recalled how "I saw that people were organizing against the logging in the Siskiyous, so I went to that. I was involved in one of the first actions by the Earth First group on Bald Mountain. We took Lou Gold up and it was very exciting, but I felt like that was something I needed to do. Back then, it was a time when people were expected to do that, they were empowered. I was a part of that time when people spoke out and acted together. This was illegal logging that was happening in the Kalmiopsis. I didn't know all the politics, I just knew I wanted to be part of trying to protect these forests. The forests basically gave me a new life. Takilma gave me a new life."

Joya and son Danya—Photo by Jim Shames

Jake and Judith Ann with daughter Molly
at the Farm-Photo by Jim Shames

PART 10

*Crimes, Protests and Problems
in the early years*

P eople came to Takilma in the summers and hung out and many filtered through, and headed for other locales, but in the end the die-hards remained through the winters and created rustic wood-heated cabins to survive the elements. One of the first challenges Takilma faced as a group was the cops coming down on them in 1969, as Delbert told in his story about early Takilma. The upshot of the televised debate was that the Governor at the time heard about all the turmoil and called the Sheriff's Dept and told them to stay out of Takilma. He told them to let the State police handle it if there is a problem. So the Liberals up north who had steered Oregon on an environmental path with their Oregon Beach Bill in 1967 and their Oregon Bottle Bill in 1971, were sticking up for the little hippie village in southern Oregon.

Another big confrontation with the law was the hippie's opposition to the aerial spraying of herbicides in the forests around Little Elder Creek in 1980. After an organized protest where people occupied the units, the Forest Service helicopters left, but they made plans to sneak in on the next Sunday morning and hand spray the units. The word got out and every horn blew, and telephones rang, and "Black Sunday" rang out with the cries of hundreds of angry hippies. After that showdown, the rangers retreated and never attempted to spray again because those types of herbicides were banned in 1984. Helen said, "We were lucky, cause no matter what they did to us, we always had someone to go in and speak for us." Delbert added with his usual wit, "Takilma is sort of a grand social experiment. Everybody comes here with their own ideas, but somehow they all get along."

This dedication to the local environment and the protection of water and other resources was uniting. People just wanted to be left alone in the peace of the forest. There were quite a few eccentric people who came to Takilma to hide out while they fulfilled a particular fantasy. One of the more unusual residents came in 1972, to buy 60 acres on the East Fork and build a "New Age Mission." The Reverend Roy Rowe, with wife Jean were preparing for a time of great calamity, in which they believed that China would detonate atom bombs and that survivors would have to be rescued by flying saucers. They even bought more land up on top of Hope Mountain where they planned to build a landing site, a church and living quarters. They had filed a lawsuit against a guy which I will call "Scorpio Man" for squatting on a mining claim up there in 1982. He failed to appear and they won, barring him from the land. After all was done, they had spent a small fortune following Jean's psychic instructions to "get a mountain and live by water. Prepare a place for training people how to use their astral bodies." Nonetheless, they lost the land up on Hope Mountain within a few years because they could not afford the taxes, and Scorpio Man reclaimed the Queen of Bronze Mine. Perhaps this was the start of a following of people who could be called survivalists. Among the more notable of these was Richard B. who collected tires and was planning to bury a jet fuel tank and create a bunker for survival in case of the apocalypse arriving. Unfortunately his plans were cut short by a fire, and subsequent condemnation of his collection of junk.

In the 70's, logging was a big part of the valley life and economy. The hippies tried to be tolerant, since they also bought wood from the mill but they didn't like the log trucks speeding through town. So one day a guy flagged a truck down and offered the guy a cold beer. He asked kindly if the guy would mind passing on a message that "the people of Takilma would appreciate it if you could slow down through here to protect people's kids and pets." The log trucks slowed down almost immediately.

In another incident, the Forest Service was going in to build a road through Hogue's Pasture, and they had their equipment ready to go, when one morning the hippies gathered round and challenged them because Hogue's Pasture is a sacred Indian site, where the Takelma Indians hunted in the old days. As Robert recounts, "They didn't want to listen to us, and it was looking bad when all of a sudden John Hoffman jumps up on a rock and shouts, Hey guys that's a terrible place to build a road-Harry, can we build it up there on the hill?" as he pointed up Bybee Gulch. They all looked up, back at the hippies and then readily agreed. So it was done, and Hogue's Meadow (as it is now called) has been treasured by the hippies ever since. It was designated as a campground, but had no toilets or facilities so sometimes campers left trash. The hippies sometimes took it upon themselves to clean the campsites, and so began a long tradition of cleaning up messes. Soon some of the hippies, led by River, started having Sufi dancing every Sunday morning in the middle of Hogue's Meadow.

This does not mean there weren't more problems to overcome. In the old days there was definitely some perceived prejudice against "the hippies" coming into town, often looking quite wild and unkempt. There were some bad elements and it seems some of the locals and shopkeepers were quite offended by and sometimes scared by these heathens. It was more than just a "generation gap" it was more like two different kinds of people getting to know each other, for the first time. It was obvious that "hippie" was a dirty word to them, and being labeled a hippie was not something too many longhairs wanted. Delbert recounts that, due to his bogus bust and subsequent meeting with the D. A. and Sheriff, he was known as the "Mayor of Takilma". "*They* may have called me that, but the people *here* didn't always agree with them", chuckles Delbert. Sometimes he had to counsel and mediate disputes and listen to hippie's stories of trouble. "It was a lot more like the Wild West back then," said Delbert. A small minority of the more "redneck types" sent their "ruffian sons" to terrorize Takilma with random incidents of beatings, shootings, fires and vandalism. In one incident some teenagers were caught harassing some naked ladies out in their garden. Another time a homemade bomb was hurled at the porch of the old Takilma store. These people may have been loosely associated with a group which formed in 1970; calling itself the "Illinois Valley Betterment Society". They printed out signs for some of the stores in Cave Junction-which proclaimed, "We do not solicit Hippie patronage".

"The authorities were always finding reasons to come out here and hassle people", said Delbert. They started sending out a guy to post signs on people's doors that they were in violation of the county building codes, and condemning their homes. The welfare department also sent people out to check on recipients living conditions and ended up taking some people's kids away. When one family turned out to be church-going rural folk, the county had to re-think their policies. It was a polarizing time and the stories about Takilma in the media at the time were really bad. Some terrible crimes had taken place, and given the hippies an even darker image.

In 1973, a group of calling itself the "Muslim Brotherhood" moved in to Takilma with mules and equipment and started to squat on Hope Mountain. Their leader McLean was a radical person who as a Muslim objected to nudity. Once he came to get Dr. Jim at gunpoint to help with a difficult birth at his home. Dr. Jim was certain that if the baby died, so would he, but he never reported the guy. One day this same fellow beat a girl who he came upon in the woods, topless. He fired a shot in the air and rode off on his horse. He was clearly menacing Black Michael, who had originally invited the man, to stay with him.

People tried to mediate the conflict, but Black Michael had packed his van and was trying to flee his mining claim in fear of his life. The Muslim leader known as Abdullah McLean had challenged him to a duel right in front of the Funky Egg Co., which led to the confrontation. Well, Abdullah was shot and killed, and the other guy taken away to jail, but it was later ruled, self-defense. Some of the people at the time said "We really don't like guns in Takilma."

In 1974, 2 grizzly murders happened, by people squatting on a mining claim on Hope Mountain. Two guys up there had thrown a crippled man in a wheelchair over a hill, and were shooting guns off at night, terrorizing the local population. Moses, as a sort of peace-keeper and spiritual leader took it upon himself to try to mediate the situation. He thought he could get through to these two young guys, who were barely twenty. One night at the Sportsman Tavern, he confronted them and told them they weren't welcome in Takilma, and why. Later after they had all been drinking, Moses and Rainbow Bob hitchhiked home with them from the bar. On their way home, along a lonely stretch of Rockydale Road, the two young desperados shot them both dead, chopped their heads off with a machete and threw them over the Waldo Bridge. It was later discovered that the murderer was an outlaw escapee from prison. This was really bad for the reputation of Takilma, even though it had nothing to do with most of the people. It was shocking and horrible. It really upset Robert, whose friend Rainbow Bob only seemed to be in the wrong place at the wrong time. At the time Robert said, "The real Takilma is so far from that crazy, violent scene."

Hippies Dancing in the field-Photo by Robert Hirning

Rainbow Bob-Photo by Robert Hirning

PART 11

Unusual People in the Early Days

Takilma in the 1970's was a decidedly more primitive place to live, but its pot smoking, groovy residents rarely seemed to have a problem getting along. Takilma was a model of peaceful co-operation. For many years, it policed itself with a band of rough looking dudes led by the likes of Takilma Nick, a Vietnam Vet.

One other Bob definitely stood out as an ikon of originality. Buckwheat Bob was a fixture of the early 70's for about 6 years, as he dropped out in Takilma and played a lot of music. Evidently he got bored of the hippie lifestyle, because he "dropped back in" after that and cut his long hair and beard and went back to a job as a computer programmer in California.

Horse Mark, was a serious throwback to the pioneer days and lived like a cowboy. He kept his horses on the flats downtown, but some days he would start out on a trip up the valley, mostly on trails he had bush whacked through the back yards of people's property. He always had two horses, one for riding and one for packing his stuff. He would ride as high up into the mountains he could go before making camp. There he would let his horses graze on the lush valley grasses and drink of the pure river water. He must have known quite a number of fine campsites high in the Siskiyous and he must have had a gun, in case of a bear encounter up there. He never had a dog, and could slip quietly by without anyone noticing. He wore a buckskin shirt sometimes and rarely spoke much. He was a real mountain man. In recent years I have not seen him passing by anymore and wonder where he has gone. I imagine he's still out there somewhere.

Takilma like any place had its share of weird and eccentric people. Everyone remembers Brett M., with the braided beard, who lived in an old bus by the Dome School, and despite being borderline crazy was tolerated for many years. His endless poems were like acid trips into the mind of a psychotic, but they were great expressions. In fact, he could recite from memory quite a variety of poems, over a page long, some longer perhaps than a patient listener could hear. He often wrote highbrow, intellectual diatribes as Letters to the Editor for the Illinois Valley News and would go into, for example, a deep philosophical analysis of the cult mentality of the Rashneeshies during the mid-80's. For a few years, he worked as an assistant to Dave K. at his glass-blowing studio. Some people really liked Brett and were very sad to see him go. However others were not too happy with his close proximity to the school, so he was asked to move his bus from behind the Dome School. He moved to Eureka, (despite Delbert's offer of a place to put his bus) and passed away a few years ago.

People also probably remember Billy WooWoo and his "Bunny", a huge bulk of a man, dressed as a woman. Perhaps it would be more politically correct to say he was a transvestite. Bunny was nobody to mess with, because she had a mean temper, and once chased a houseload of meth-heads out of lower Takilma. Legend has it that she burned their house down. (But that's a story better left unsaid). Billy was a gentle poet who wrote, emphatic poems, of his grandiose passion for Takilma. Here is an excerpt from one of his many poems.

> "Made in Takilma
> Heard that song before,
> It'll play on the radio
> When it does, open up your door
> Take down the barrier and un-fold
> The peace that Takilma (indeed) makes
> Will leave all of us
> Continually begging for more
> *MAKE LOVE*"

Another one of Billy's famous poems was a song about the

> **Longwood-Takilma Fire**.
> It was September in Takilma
> And the woods were bone dry
> When all at once, we got attacked by
> lightning from the sky.
> "Sheriff, don't take us away!"
> The crops that were a 'growin
> Lay hidden on the lands

And soon would be cut down anyway, by
the Sheriff's heavy hand
"Sheriff, don't take us away!"
Well he said he would cut them down and
he didn't blink an eye,
When on that day, the Devil let rip, pink
ladies from the sky.
"Sheriff, don't take us away!"
You know the fire came from the
lightening
And what do you do about that?
But calling us criminals for growin and
smokin
Is the biggest sin ever perpetrated
As meanwhile the Devil kept on stoking
the horrible Takilma fire.
"Sheriff, don't take us away!"
We'll call for a successful resolution to this
question
And then we'll all be tokin, we'll have a
Pow-Wow session
And then we'll be stoking our peace pipes
and our minds
(Yeah, hand that joint down the line, and
save the race of mankind.)
While we're livin on the land and we're
doin the best we can.
So "Sheriff, don't take us away!"
From the "Takilma Aviator" a newsletter
where the "truth will out!"

Billy, a former Air Force Veteran from Mendocino
County, whose job it once was to guard a nuclear

arsenal, developed a clinical case of paranoia and was honorably discharged. After traveling the world three times he settled down to a life in the Haight-Ashbury district of California, where he laid claim to being one of the original hippies. He became a Poet, Herbalist and the owner of a business called Aud-Vid Productions. His observations of drug use in America were prefaced by the statement that he did NOT use illicit drugs, however "in reality, there is nothing at all morally wrong with a person's taking of certain drug agents. The Police and the politicians have perpetrated this myth."

Otis, a good natured and loveable big drunk, was a fixture of downtown Takilma after his wife Kitty died, and he inherited the "little red house in Takilma." He wore his long dreads and black leathers for many years, on his daily bicycle trips to town. Otis was in and out of trouble over the years and once he was found sleeping on the floor of Hammer's Market after he broke in to steal some stuff. Apparently he was so tired after the stress of breaking in and eating his fill, he fell asleep on the floor and was arrested the next morning. In later years he would be the cause of several arrests for swerving into traffic and being drunk. I think he spent a year in jail after one incident. After that he was reformed and wore a bike light and bright reflective vest for safety.

Pumba, his friend, who used to go barefoot all year long, finally had to move to town one winter. White Fox, used to have the unfortunate habit of falling asleep on the side of the road, where any unwary driver might have to swerve to avoid hitting him. One day, his luck ran out.

I'm certain that for several years, there was a group of drug users, who were definitely just living an outlaw existence on the edges of Takilma, living in old busses and hide-outs. So they were always in and out of trouble with the law, and perhaps that's the side of Takilma that very few know about. The shadowy, dark underside of Takilma consisted of those outlaws who had succumbed to drug and alcohol addiction. Many of them grew and sold pot to support their habits, and due to the inflated prices of the black market, they were able to do so. Many of those people sadly are no are no longer with us.

The early 80's were a time when there were many pot busts, and raids (as described earlier, in Jim's story of how the Fire Station got built) and over 50 people from the Illinois Valley were arrested and taken to jail, during a period of a few months. The Sheriff at the time, was on a "get tough on crime" agenda. A guy by the name of "Roger" had gotten off some weapons charges by agreeing to become a snitch. He went around soliciting hippies to sell him pot. So many did get pulled in with his informing, but due to his reprehensible tactics 34 of the cases were thrown out of court. The others were felons who went off to prison. There was no more casual cultivation of pot and the problems that went with it. It might be said that Takilma got cleaned up, and the people still growing pot were a lot more careful after that time. The yearly fly-overs of planes and helicopters looking for pot fields continued and made people paranoid. Takilma sort of sounded like a war zone sometimes.

Everything changed in the late 90's when Medical Marijuana was legalized in Oregon. People could get a license to grow their own cannabis for medicinal uses, and since southern Oregon is eminently suited to its cultivation, many did avail themselves of this opportunity. The freedom from paranoia and fear was a blessing and the right to use their medicine of choice was something that the older hippies valued after years of persecution. Today Takilma is still in the forefront of major changes in American society. Their liberal values and new ideas are pushing the envelope.

Many hippies were hemp activists who believed that the legalization of hemp and cannabis would revolutionize the world's economies and bring prosperity back to the middle class in America. The world's forests were being depleted at an alarming rate and the hippies believed that growing hemp for fuel, fiber, building materials, paper, rope, and other industrial uses would save the forests, and eventually even the world from global warming. The trail was blazed for this new way of living in Takilma, where people believed in a new economy emerging in a timber dependent area, with little or no agriculture except vineyards. The days of making a living mining and logging were fast dwindling away.

Carrying on the outlaw tradition on Hope Mountain, Scorpio Man was a shadowy character, who lived on the Queen of Bronze mining claim and was as wily as a fox, in his deleterious actions which were often the talk of the town. One gentle man, a poet and writer for the Illinois Valley News by the name of Adrian, who lived below Scorpio Man's place, was in constant fear of him until he left the community, presumably to find some peace of mind. Scorpio Man went on to a long career of threatening people. With training as a paralegal he knew how to create quite legal looking documents. He and his thugs were often suspected of vandalism and outlaw activity in the back woods. Rumor had it that Scorpio Man, in later years, was the victim of a shooting and an arson that burned down his place on Hope Mountain.

Another mysterious character was Robert P., a big city cat who bought up all the land he could around Takilma and then became a high rolling tycoon, selling off his land and logging the big trees out whenever the taxes were due. He and his neighbors didn't always get along.

Some of the most pressing problems were getting supplies to the remote places and carrying building supplies up into the hills on bad roads. Many people had old cars and few resources to draw from. Many had to resort to going on welfare if times were tough. Others were determined to be self reliant. In 1972, the hippies led by Patrick F. who had come up from San Francisco, devised a way to get food to Takilma. As Libby recounts, "In the old days Patrick would go to the Bay Area or Portland to pick up supplies of bulk foods for the hippies in Takilma, and store it in Alice and Richard H.'s shed." Alice, who lived on a hill, was a free-spirited flower child from San Francisco, who became one of the long-term residents of Takilma. As Libby continued, "Soon the supplies could not fit in there anymore, and then we opened the store in Wonder. Patrick and I ran the health food store in Wonder for three years. We had a guy Jerry who helped in the summers and made soup and sandwiches to sell out of the extra produce. Then health food stores opened in Grants Pass and Takilma, and we closed down and moved to Takilma to join the new Takilma Food Cooperative." It operated out of the store location downtown for a short period in the late 70's but the absentee owner of the building refused to renew the lease just after a considerable amount of community free labor had been expended to fix up the property. Lila kicked out the Takilma Food Co-op so she could run her little operation of selling beer and brownies. From then on the TFC operated out of the Dome School which eventually got a commercial kitchen for the school. The cooperative spirit and networking of the hippies was a big success with the TFC. There were up to 40 families and communes which ordered their food bulk and volunteered to break it down every two weeks at the new community building.

A guy named Dustin bought the store location from the owner Lila in 1980 and started another small store in downtown Takilma. He ran the store for five years, making a living at his jumble of general goods even though it didn't seem to fit in. In 1985, he was arrested for shooting and killing a guy named Jimmy in front of his store. The story was; Jimmy was threatening him because of his propositioning boys at the store. After the shooting, Dustin did some time, but there was an element of self-defense which allowed the judge to grant him an early release; soon after Dustin died of AIDS. By then the store had burned down, presumably by arson, and the former owner had re-possessed the land again. (The first time the Takilma Store burned down was in 1974, when Lila let her fire get out of hand. The assistant Fire Chief was injured in that fire when the roof collapsed.)

Finally Lila, sold it to a Native American; Dale V. who bought the lot which had nothing left but a cement slab over a septic tank. It was a clear slate, after being burned down, and cleared off. Dale decided to change all that bad karma and bring back some good energy to downtown Takilma. Over the next ten years he re-built the commercial building there, in hopes of someday having a traditional native Longhouse, and small general store to meet the community's needs. His presence has re-connected the Native American spirit to the heart of Takilma and allowed a renaissance of energy to heal the land and restore the town.

Buckwheat on the Road '71

Buckwheat Bob in the 1970's. Photo
courtesy of Robert Hirning

Takilma Food Cooperative in 1980-Photo
courtesy of Robert Hirning

PART 12

The Takilma Community Building

C harley G. came in 1974 from the Silicon Valley, with a degree in Engineering. He and his young family were looking for a place to live. His grandfather had told him he ought to visit Takilma and his friends, Lou and Margaret. Turns out Charley ended up buying their land; the first place he came to. He recalled, "I came here to work on my human-powered car project. My goal was to find someplace that was so far off the radar that I could do all of my experiments and whittle away at it, and not have to deal with the regular world." Charley was fortunate to have studied stress analysis and was able to adapt his knowledge to an early computer software program. So this led him to advance. He was able to help with the engineering of the first tree houses, using this early technology. Charley said, "All of a sudden it turned out it was the best way to solve trees."

Charley's different cars and machines are all around him in his workshop and he reflects; "For me it's been a long, long coordinated movement, like stuff

I started doing in the 60's is physically still here with me now; parts, designs, skills, you keep building. Until I punch my ticket, it's always a continuum." In regards to his "Human-Powered" car, Charley has been all over to show it. He says, "It's like street theatre, it makes people think outside the box. You can really feel the power of the other people when you are driving it. Some people would tell us, we don't think you can do that!" referring to how some car producers might have been a bit "scared" by the idea of a car with no need of gasoline. In fact his cars have the ability to generate their own electricity. Charley adds, "People from the city would come here and they couldn't even imagine what we were doing here, so we got used to it." Nowadays, Charley's son Chuck is his business partner and he feels a real family groove will continue.

Charley was also one of the rock stars of Takilma. He describes how he learned to play in the 50's and joined the musician's union in the 60's. He said, "I caught that whole wave, Surf music, then the English music, and I also did some recording for Fantasy Records." It helped put him through college, playing at smaller venues; however Charley stopped short of signing a contract. So after moving to Takilma, Charley played with groups like the "Siskiyou Kids", "Steelhead", "Joyce's Kitchen" and "Rock Robin and the Toasters". He said, "From then on I did it all for fun. We built that community building and I did the heating system, the hydro-electric system and the engineering of the trusses. We played a gazillion benefits. There are a lot of wonderful memories."

The New Dome School was built in 1983 on land which was formerly owned by Longview Timber

Company. The Green Side up crew did some thinning jobs for them in exchange for the land and volunteers donated their pay. Teams of hippies were forming to clear the land and build a community building. A non-profit was formed for the Dome School, as the primary user of the building. Using the best talents of Takilma, and the donations of its citizens, the building went up fairly quickly. Charley recalls having to do the engineering on a whole other level, "We had to pre-drill, insert and cleat 30,000 nails into a very specific pattern. So the day came to install 31 trusses and Frank said, 'let's just try it!' So we got 10 or 15 people and passed them up, one by one." The feat of building such a large and complex structure to code is a lasting achievement of the people of Takilma. The Dome School has been operating since then, providing quality education to children from all over the Illinois Valley. By the same token, the Takilma Community Building has operated simultaneously, hosting numerous events and community functions.

From its humble beginnings in Takilma, The Takilma People's Clinic moved to Cave Junction in 1989, where it took over the old offices of a medical practitioner. From there changed its name to the Siskiyou Community Health Center. In a few years it outgrew its location, and obtained a federal grant to expand services. With the help of several large grants a new facility was built five years ago, north of Cave Junction on the Redwood Highway. Today it is still growing there and serving the entire Illinois Valley. The year 2013 is the 40th Anniversary of the small Clinic which started in Takilma. Sue, who is now a Physician's Assistant has worked there all those years, and she says, "Some of my patients are the grandchildren of kids I've delivered." And the SCHC, is expanding soon, to include a new dental clinic, 3 new providers, an outreach building and a pharmacy. It proudly remains one of the largest employers in the Illinois Valley.

Dr. Jim and his wife Heidi, after ensuring the success of the new medical center in Cave Junction, were one of those families who moved away for a better education for their children and better employment advances to their careers. Dr. Jim; now the Director of the Jackson and Josephine County Health Departments, still keeps his family's home and their connection to Takilma. Dr. Jim, with his hobby of photography, has published a book of old photos from the early days in Takilma, and some of these are featured in this book. Dr. Jim took the various group photos of the entire Takilma community in front of the Forge, three times over the last 30 years. All the proceeds from their sales were donated back to the Dome School.

Dr. Jim's success in health care was rewarded in 2013 by the State of Oregon when he received the award for Doctor of the Year.

Sheila recalls that, "A lot of the people that worked at the Clinic; medical people, have gone on and become some of the best Dr's, PA's and nurses at the tops in their fields. They are all these magnificent, over-qualified professionals." When asked what she liked most about working at the Clinic, Sheila said, "It was very good in the sense of learning about diversity in people. It was just another chapter for me. It wasn't just about Takilma, when we did health care, it was about people. I don't care if you're a logger or a hippie. There are no labels in health care. That was one of the gems that came out of it; diversity." So Sheila went on to talk about how the Clinic helped to bring the Illinois Valley people together on many levels. "When you live in a tight community, sometimes you shut yourself off from other people, you get polarized, so it's really good when all of a sudden you have to take your idea and really be honest with it, and all those righteous things go out the door. It's not necessary."

The women of Takilma endured special challenges. People celebrated a simple lifestyle, yet living in primitive conditions and raising children in the early days were part of learning to survive. Women's personal stories are as rich with the terrible tragedies of miscarriages, stillbirth, abortion, pre-mature babies, disease and accidental death, as they are rich with the beauty of labor, childbirth and healthy kids. Besides that, they had to deal with health issues and birth control. Women had to do the hard work of raising kids and sometimes the cost fell on their shoulders too as single mothers. Some women had to deal with divorce, poverty and other social problems, yet throughout the history of Takilma, women have risen up as leaders, rooted to the land. They have held on to the deeds, and fiercely protected their lands. Women's liberation is alive and well in Takilma, where women have taken on all roles, from hard-riding horse ranchers to piano teachers. Hippies, being quite open minded about divorce, would often allow their partner to just move across the street or next door, rather than upset the kids. This liberal attitude by parents, to stay friendly, even in divorce helped the children adjust, and didn't force anyone out. The assistance of the Takilma People's Clinic was immeasurable to the hippie women of Takilma during the 1970's and 80's giving them the security and support they needed to survive.

Many of the hippies of Takilma were being integrated into the fabric of the southern Oregon and finding employment and lasting relationships with people outside of their core friendships and broadening their horizons, so to speak. Very few, though have chosen to cut their ties to Takilma. Most always plan on coming home. Sue said that, "For me the biggest reward of working in a small town is just knowing people for so long, helping them and knowing what they are going through." Sheila added that, "I'm very proud that there's still health care in the valley. Not only has it survived, but it is still growing! I see generations going down that path, and that part's really wonderful."

The Takilma Community Building under
construction-Photo by Jim Shames

The Takilma Community Building and Dome School
workday with volunteers-Photo by Robert Hirning

PART 13

The Longwood Fire of 1987

D uring the Longwood Fire of 1987, the Clinic in the TCA building in Takilma was used as a headquarters and an emergency coordination site for medical help. The date of August 30, 1987 was the infamous date of that storm, when lightning struck the ridge top. It was a huge crisis in the history of Takilma, as the residents were asked to evacuate, and they were also galvanized to fight the fires themselves because the air tankers were going to be 3 days late on other fires. Residents could see the flames coming down both sides of the canyons, and were asked to take their valuables with them.

Crews of local volunteers were quick to spring into action and gathered all their resources. The call had gone out and the rest of the Illinois Valley responded with lightning speed. Within a few hours 40 trucks arrived and these residents backed their trucks up to the clinic driveway, opened their trunks and just dropped off their chain saws, gas tanks, tools, and other supplies. Carl Hammer literally emptied his shelves and brought the stuff out. Some women from town came out and made sack lunches for the crews and T.a. went out on horseback to deliver them to the guys on the line.

People had hastily thrown valuables into trucks and trailers and taken children to safe areas. Some, like Della had dropped her valuables including her piano into an open field down by the road. There she played some music to while away the hours. Others defied orders and stayed on to water down their roofs and around their homes. The smoke was quite thick and intense to breath.

The staging area was set up at Dave K's field, up on the Cook Ranch. The fire was fought from there by volunteers, over about a week's time. "It started when the Forest Service showed up and just started bringing trucks into my field", said Dave K. "Soon a procurement team came in to rent the space and asked me to put a sign up because all the rigs were missing the place. All of the workers would come and gather and then send the cats and crews out on the line. After three days busses showed up with out of state firefighters, but you couldn't stop the volunteer effort. Twenty guys worked all night building a fire line behind my house."

When all was done the fire had burned over 10,000 acres all around the community. Only the BLM plantation of old growth timber was left standing. The old Aller Mining Claim log cabin was the only structure burned and no lives were lost. Rumor had it that the lightning storm hit some logging equipment that was left out on the ridge top, and that is what caused the fire. The heavy smoke lingered over the

Takilma valley for many weeks after that as the people painfully put their lives back together.

It was quite a relief to know that everyone was OK and had survived the disaster. Only the land looked pained and black; the hillsides naked and barren of the trees which had flourished there for so long. Takilma, as a community had reached the critical moment of big changes and a warning about nature's fury. It had also reached a place of relief in knowing their homes and their small community was safe. The acceptance generated when the town reached out to help built some strong bridges. From then on there was much less of an "us and them" feeling.

People could feel that the people from town cared about them and that fact was brought home by the new Pastor in Takilma, Pastor Dan Robinson. As Sherry Lou recalls, "Some older men in Cave Junction were praying for Takilma every day and wanting to see a church built in Takilma. They knew of the American Missionary Fellowship and that they plant churches in rural towns as their mission. Dan was a missionary and was asked if he would pray about coming to Takilma. He could not get away from the calling. He really connected with the people of the valley during the fire of 87." From then on Pastor Dan joined in the efforts to open the Takilma Bible Church and to be its minister. Sherry Lou and her family joined the church, after hearing from a friend that "Pastor Dan is amazing! You gotta try this church!" Sherry Lou and Michael's daughter, Star later married Pastor Dan and today they have a happy family of six daughters and one son. Pastor Dan is always looking to find ways he can help people in the community and "does all he is called to do" for the people.

The Longwood Fire of 1987-Photo
courtesy of Robert Hirning

Fire volunteers and community people at the
Clinic-Photo courtesy of Robert Hirning

Randall with Forest Service workers-
Photo by Robert Hirning

PART 14

The Out n About Treehouse Resort

Michael G. had the inspired vision of making money off the trees by not cutting them down, when he "assumed those Fantasy Flakes" in 1978. Gemini Bill came up with the name, and Michael created the box of "The Ethereal Serial-Breakfast of Geniuses." Michael built a prototype of his "Picture Propeller" out of wood and took it to the Renaissance Faire, where it fired up people's imagination. Michael had tried to make a living tree planting, horse logging, and as a medic but he found he didn't have quite the temperament for internal medicine. He was more of an emergency medic. As Michael remembers, "People wanted to be fixed, so I went back 100 years and created a feel good bottle. The main remedy was a song, a dance and laughter. I saw the magic and myth of medicine and decided to become a "MDGQ; a Mighty Damn Good Quack." So that was the birth of the Dr. Birch's Medicine Show which Michael performed for several years and even took on the road to the Four Corners of the West.

Michael's Medicine Shows and plays were some of the most memorable events in the valley. He and Charley Two Shoes had a Laurel and Hardy act which could split your sides with belly laughs. The ragtime piano playing by Dave K. and troupe of can-can dancers made it one hell of a show.

In 1985 he partnered with Richard H. of Bright Star productions and put on an old fashioned melodrama called "Dirty Works at the Crossroads" at the old theatre in Cave Junction. Michael played the villain Murgatroyd, to poor, sweet Nellie who was tied to the railroad tracks in one of the most realistic scenes ever created in such a small play. The house was packed with enthusiastic hippies, but it was later learned that some were arrested outside for unknown reasons. Still the show went on and Nellie was saved.

In later years, Michael co-wrote a play called "Where's Waldo", about the wild, west history of the gold rush town of Waldo and had a troupe of hippies perform it at the Lions Labor Day event, on a temporary stage, where it inspired wild enthusiasm from the crowd.

So Michael continues with his story, "I came here for medicine but the valley needed a source of income and people needed better living conditions. I kept trying different things. I wanted to make a living off living trees." He built the first tree house for his kids and it was a hit. In 1990 he re-built the Peacock House with Doug K's design and started renting it out as a bed and breakfast. "I put metal on the tree and then wood on the metal. It was different." He saw that it could make money. He added, "All the things that didn't work are a part of it now, but it was the tree houses that made it happen. People really enjoyed themselves, and it was like preventative medicine; very relaxing on a beautiful piece of property. I liked building things and success is being able to afford making a living at what you like to do." Slowly, one by one the different tree houses were built, and now the "Treesort" is sold out each summer season and provides many jobs for locals. It is a place where "tree-history" sort-of started, with the development of the resort and its attractions. Today it has 15 unique and different treehouses, and hosts activities like hiking, rafting, horse-back riding and zip lines.

Every 4th of July Out 'n About sponsors the annual Takilma slow-pitch softball game, down on Michael's lower field. This event always starts at noon, as players are chosen for the teams, called the Tater Heads and the Geezers. This often comical and amazing spectacle (pitting young bravado against the wisdom of experience) is very well attended by hippie regulars and lots of summer visitors. It is followed that evening by a huge 4th of July spectacular fireworks show and outdoor dance concert. This event has gotten bigger every year and attracts people from all over the region. Nobody can doubt that the Treesort is a groovy place and adds to the stability of Takilma. More information on the resort is found at www.treehouses.com.

In fact Michael G's vision has expanded in the years since his Treesort became popular, to helping others succeed as well. He helped long time friend Sandy L. get into the bed and breakfast business by helping her build the "Lily Pad" treehouse in the tall trees on her land. Now she can earn a living without leaving home and the Treesort helps to book her treehouse with visitors all year long. These kind of collaborations have always been a strength of the people of Takilma where they have always been helpful to their neighbors.

The people of Takilma had always come together to work on issues they cared about and took steps which were innovative. In 1983, after a community meeting in which the residents were polled, 70% of the population of Takilma voted yes on a TCA resolution to create a Nuclear-Free Zone in Takilma. They were the first community in Josephine County, and perhaps the whole country, to do this.

In 1984, many of the same people marched through the streets of Cave Junction on a Peace March sponsored by the Women's Initiative for Peace, to bring attention to the continuing cost and escalation of wars across the world. Since then a group called "Women in Black" have been standing for peace each Monday at noon in front of the Josephine County Building to express their opposition to war in a peaceful, silent manner.

The idea of a Blackberry Festival started long ago, in the 80's when two businessmen in Cave Junction, Les L. and Jim F., found out that Holland boasted the longest continuous blackberry hedge in Oregon and as such deserved some special recognition. So to boost their sales in mid-August they proposed a street fair where vendors would mingle their wares with those of the business people, who could bring a table to the sidewalk. This kind of shameless promotion was made fun with blackberry jam, jelly and pie contests. The Blackberry Festival has survived as an event which still helps support small businesses, and craftspeople in Cave Junction. In recent years, the Illinois River Valley Arts Council has sponsored a monthly Artwalk event which showcases artwork and music in Cave Junction businesses.

The Takilma Community Building continues to provide a venue and a focal point, not only for the Dome School but for all of the residents of the area. Parties can rent the space and the kitchen facilities, because the school furniture is on rollers and can be moved for multiple uses. Katherine continues to work at the Dome School as a teacher and takes people out on tours in the summer. She reveals her feelings, "This is a very special area. I take people on horseback tours at Out 'n About in the summers, and people are amazed at this area. We are stewards of this area. I've spent many years hiking, and I've lived here so long now, I feel like I am the forest. I've found so much satisfaction here, I'm never bored and the beauty always amazes me."

The first treehouse called the Peacock House-
Photo courtesy of Michael Garnier

Dr Birch's Medicine Show with Brian Bones and
Calamity Jane-photo by Robert Hirning

Miguelo on the Geezer team at the 4th of July
Celebration-photo by Robert Hirning

The Out 'n About Treehouse Stress Test-
photo by Robert Hirning

PART 15

Making Dreams Come True

K atherine from Sun Star remembers how she overcame her financial challenges in Takilma. "First I was a cook at Captain Mike's restaurant and ever since I've been working at the Dome School over twenty years. Actually I continued to work on my college degree for many years and ended up getting my degree from Eastern Oregon University. My mother was a teacher in the East Bay. We toured Montessori schools throughout Italy, and lived there for about a year. So later I taught in the Bay area with her, in her schools. So I've brought those skills to The Dome School. The Dome School is a school for people that want to be involved with their children and it's a place for our community to be involved, to have a chance to interact. We have such a variety of age groups. We are so rich, in talent, education and knowledge and experience. So that's why we are such a rich school, because we draw constantly from our community. It never fails."

Katherine, helps put on the Martin Luther King Day benefit every year for the Dome School, and explains why she does it, "I am a person of culture. I am attracted to and reach out to and facilitate and celebrate culture. So whoever has some traditions to share, and different insights to share; that's something that I really go after. That we have children as the center of our community, I think is what keeps us inspired and young and strong."

"We always studied Martin Luther King Day in school and the civil rights era was a big part of my growing up; non violence and civil disobedience. These were the highlights of our lives; celebrating environmental and social diversity. This is what our generation got to participate in. Martin Luther King continues to inspire me and be relevant. This is going be our 7th year, of doing this event with the children and they especially love the story of Harriet Tubman and Rosa Parks, and a lot of the women that were part of the movement. Rosa Parks started the whole freedom movement. So we go through the speeches of Martin Luther King and we have been singing songs with Libby, about the Underground Railroad and it brings up a lot of important questions that we discuss. So the children have a chance to perform, memorize and sing songs. It's just a good social studies theme in American history. We also give to a small charity in Zimbabwe, and talk to the kids that there are people who have less that us. So we have been sending, when we can, support to this little school in Africa. We've had many different artists coming in to teach our kids."

Katherine believes in the people here and the future. She's given everything that she has to give. And she feels that Takilma has given her back so much more honor. She believes in cooperatives and thinks more people should form land co-operatives. She implores the children to "Keep this Dream Alive!!" Looking back she remembers all the achievements of Takilma. "We did the unimaginable. We made it and we are doing it all. We even die here. All we need is our own little cemetery."

Another lady summed up her love for Takilma in one sentence, "I was enthralled every day, with the beauty and the people." I think that sentiment was shared by many of the residents.

One of the most unusual and successful art ventures from Takilma was called the "Illuminated Fools" a giant puppet troupe created by Newman and a group of friends. Newman, a mask-maker by trade created a variety of larger-than-life puppets built on the frames of back-packs which people could wear and perform in. His archetypal puppets represented universal characters which helped to communicate messages to the public, whilst being visually stunning. His puppets were the most exciting part of many of the Takilma dances and other events over the years. He also dabbled in performing "Shadow Puppetry" on evenings of outdoor theatre, with children and adults enjoying this ancient art form.

Newman, River and many others, involved people in another one of his art forms, by having lantern making workshops. He would bring all the cedar wood and paper mache materials and people would get very creative with making a variety of old fashioned lanterns. There were stars, moons, planets and fantastical sculptures of figures and animals. Then on a special Solstice Night the people would parade from the Dome School around the downtown area with these magical candle lit lanterns which glowed gold in the darkness. These ancient ways of celebrating the earth cycles and coming together in a tribal way, were what made Takilma a magical and uplifting place to be and the sight of the lantern parade floating through Takilma looked like an illuminated dragonfly; quite endearing, colorful and inviting. As Jill T. said, "We did stick, because we became indigenous!"

Jill T., one of Newman's first apprentices, who first lived in a tipi at Talsalsan, was helping make the costumes for the puppets. In her early years Jill and her friends (with the help of Kerry H.) snuck into the Oregon Country Faire and were invited to perform all weekend. She recalls, "We joined the Risk of Change and met Leo DeFlambo who is the giant puppet maestro on the West Coast. He made the first giant puppet at the Oregon Country Faire. Then Newman made some giant puppets and he asked me if I would make some costumes and hair for them." It was a magical introduction to the performing arts in Oregon.

Jill, who was with the Fools for 13 years, remembers how it all started, "At first it was me and Mike, Newman and Rebecca. We bought the Fools Bus, an old church bus and 'Hippieized it.' We had many amazing adventures in that bus, up and down the West Coast. We started doing Political Theatre pretty quickly with things like 'A Fairy Tale' among many others and also a play called 'Give Trees a Chance' which was about logging greed vs ecology." Jill went on to recall some of the highlights of those early years, working with the Fools. "We worked with the kids a lot. The Oregon Country Faire hired us to make all these bird costumes for the kids. Cirque du Soliel called us to perform with them in Portland and then we got to attend their cast party afterwards. We did lots of pageants and festivals. Oh and we were part of the Millenium Celebration in Portland, that was really big and then we were performing at festivals like Reggae on the River every year."

After going through a branching off from the Fools and her first husband Mike, Jill decided to break away from the Fools and to create her own business, called "Coyote Rising." As a busy mother with a family to support, she still was able to take on her own gigs at events and attended innumerable ceremonies. The main character of her new line of puppets started with "Coyote; the Trickster" which she made in 1989. Jill says, "The Coyote symbolizes the Trickster, or child spirit, who can do whatever he wants." Jill also started a craft of creating and selling hand-made authentic Native American style rattles, which she takes with her to all of her shows. As her new business evolved, she was able to add many more puppet figures to her line-up, including, SUN puppet, Mother Earth, Rasta Man, the Dragonfly, the Mushrooms, the Trees and Tri-Zorg the three-headed Alien, to name a few. With five sewing machines and lots of people and materials to organize, it was not an easy undertaking to run Coyote Rising. Jill recalls, "It continues to be fun and a huge part of my life. I've been teaching people at a "Gaia Workshop" where they can build their own puppet. I love teaching my skills and seeing people put their own art on them." Some of Jill's biggest helpers have brought their own unique skills into her art, such as Frank A. who was really involved with all the behind the scenes production for a long time. Currently Albert F. is helping with fabrication and design. Jill is clearly happy in her life of bringing joy to people through her art. She says, "I'm comfortable with eccentricity. I like colorful people. I've lived communally more than ever and I like the energy. I like people who are comfortable being themselves in my space. The hippie community of Takilma is my soul, my comfort, it feeds me. It's family-my tribe-and gives me a deep spiritual connection."

This deep spiritual connection to the land is what seems to bring out the passionate loyalty in most of the valley residents. They love their beautiful and quiet corner of the earth and want it to retain its rural qualities. The stewardship that people feel for the Klamath Siskiyou bio-region is evident in the strong bond of neighbors and friends helping each other.

Sometimes a big issue brought all sides together to oppose something nobody wanted. Such was the case of a Prison proposal that was brought to Cave Junction in 1996 by a company which planned to buy an old farm on Rockydale Rd. and turn it into a 1,600 bed, minimum security prison. This plan was huge and would have dramatically impacted the local community. People under the leadership of Dave Toler and others banded together, to form the Rockydale Association to oppose the plans. Their supporters grew to over 500 people and filled the IV High School auditorium on one occasion with impassioned speakers, and people from both sides of the aisle united in opposition. They were able to stop the development and within a decade, Dave Toler was elected as Josephine County Commissioner. Takilma finally had one of their own rise to prominence in public office. Later, Dave Toler was also instrumental in writing a grant to build the Senior Center and another grant for the Takilma Community Building kitchen addition and ADA bathrooms.

Other bridges were built through the opportunities for people to further their education during the Clinton years. There were grants to go back to college and many did avail themselves of further classes in their chosen careers. Robert got his plumber's license, and went on to open Country Plumbing which has served the IV for over 30 years. Delbert took the opportunity to expand his business to town, when he opened Kauffman Wood Products, in Kerby. Kerry W. opened an alternative energy company, called Energy Outfitters which installs solar and hydro energy systems. The economy was thriving in the 90's, and many people found jobs and more prosperity.

Guys like Lance and Kenny built an overseas dream in Mexico; they are the perennial travelers of Takilma who travel to warmer climates each winter. Another group of people migrated to Hawaii's Big Island, where they found cheap land, not unlike in Oregon. Some like Newman eventually joined a new culture. He is now a resident of Bali, after he traveled there to learn more about mask-making. Others have professional careers which take them away on adventures like Jenny May, a vibrant singer and actress who teaches music to many Takilma kids and adults. Her husband Menno, is the manager of the Oregon

Caves Chateau, and is involved in many projects of economic betterment for the Illinois Valley.

Doug K. opened his own building design business in 1978. Since then he has designed or remodeled over 500 projects in the IV. His projects have graced the town of Cave Junction from Dave's Outdoor, to Carlo's Restaurant, to Radio Shack to Wild River Pizza, adding immeasurably to the beauty of our town. He has also developed plans for Out 'n About tree houses, including Michael G.'s personal residence. In the earlier days he volunteered to design and draft plans and remodels for the present day Dome School/ Community Building where he continues to serve on the Build Committee Advisory Board.

Jim R. is now much more than the village blacksmith. He is the artistic director of the Jefferson Baroque Orchestra, a group of people with a passion for ancient musical instruments and the music of Johann Sebastian Bach. His group performs a variety of composers from the Baroque time period. Jim, who is known for his blacksmith work featured in the "Pirates of the Caribbean" movies, also helped make some unique brooms for the Harry Potter movies. He has spent over 520 days at sea on the *Lady Washington*, an old sailing ship anchored in Washington State. He recently accepted his Captain's License, and a position on a ship called the *Royaliste*. Surprisingly, when asked about his greatest achievement, Jim is proudest of all the durable hardware he has created to grace people's homes.

Things really changed quickly in Takilma during the 90's. You could say it was because people's kids were growing up in the local schools and getting to know the other kids in the town. Maybe you could conjecture that it was the kids that all played sports together since they were little kids that made people come together. It may have been during the years that the boy's basketball team went to the State championship or maybe it was the year when the girl's basketball team went to State, but there were many games when the entire town turned out and cheered the house down in wild enthusiasm. Those were times when people looked down the bleachers and saw their neighbors and realized that they were all on the same side. It was a great feeling of pride and acceptance.

That was also true when some of the hippie kids became the valedictorian's of the Illinois Valley High School. Russell, Helen and Delbert's son, was the first one to achieve the honor in 1980 and went on to earn a degree in High Energy Particle Physics at Stanford University. Since then he has taught college physics and now works for an aerospace company. Certainly, since then Takilma has had a surprisingly large group of high achieving students. The valley is replete with many success stories of the hippie's children who went on to great lives away from home, yet who still appreciate their upbringing in Takilma. As Delbert recalled, "It was a great environment for raising kids, because everybody in the community took an interest in the kids. They do a pretty good job at the Dome School. There have been a remarkable number of Dome School students that end up at the head of the class at Illinois Valley High School."

Some of those Dome School graduates have gone on to careers as varied as manager of Eco-Haus Business, Biology Consultant for Watershed Health,

Dental Health Director, Lawyer, Whitewater River Guide, Registered Nurse, Renewable Energy System designer, Dome School teacher and environmental educator.

As these young people face different challenges out in the world they will create networks and friendships which help them succeed. The way they were raised perhaps is a great advantage to them because it gave them such a caring relationship to their families and a big community to fall back on. They definitely have made everyone proud.

Coyote the Trickster-a Giant Puppet created by Jill T.
Photo by Kindi Fahrnkopf

Belly Dancing at the Hope Mountain Barter
Faire-Photo by Kindi Fahrnkopf

Katherine teaching at the Dome School-
Photo by Katherine Roncalio

PART 16

Music in Takilma

During the summers, today as well as in years past, people gathered at various swimming holes along the East Fork of the Illinois to cool off and take their afternoon breaks. The river was a big part of life and the free exchange of ideas gave rise to many Takilma friendships. Most people went naked in the old days; some still do. People brought their arts and crafts to work on as they kept cool under the trees. As Maya recalls, "We spent the long, hot hours of the summer at the swim hole, along Paco's land, with Annie, Jim and many horses, and Jane, Michael, Joe and Eli across the river. We all sang to our babes and especially the women had a lot of closeness. What we shared was unspoken, yet profound. We learned by association 'how we do what we do,' this mothering in a more natural, organic, loving basis." The joys of a pleasant afternoon on a pebbly beach with friends and families, and clear cold water to swim in, with soft acoustic music wafting through the trees and the sound of children laughing, were some of the best pastimes of the early days.

Takilma does have many incredible musicians and it seems that one cannot find anyone without some sort of musical talent. The many events and parties of the past will no doubt live on in the memories of the hippies, as some of the best times of their lives. Monthly full moon parties became a tradition where people would share and teach each other their songs and music was practiced. Different types of music, like Folk, Bluegrass, Indian, Marimbas, Reggae, acoustic Rock and Rap were developed and drum circle groups have flourished, as well as belly-dancing and other forms of expression. There were so many great events like the time Clan Dyken came and pulled their solar bus up to the TCA land and gave Takilma a fantastic concert, with a blanket dance benefiting the Dine Navaho people.

During the 80's and 90's there were several big dances each year, and apart from hosting a lot of other groups to the stage, the regulars like Charley's group, Rock Robin and the Toasters were the ones to dance to. Charley's particular type of guitar playing, brought together the best of the hard-driving rock rhythms with the more intricate lead guitar riffs which made the music so irresistible for dancers. In more recent years Charley plays with Kenny, Donny, and Dave M. in another great dance band named Altered States.

Another hugely popular dance group was the Toyes. Mawg and his brother Sky started the group and wrote their first big hit in Hawaii. "Smoke Two Joints" became an overnight sensation and was recorded for the first time in 1982. Over the years, the Toyes performed at many annual events including Out 'n About's summer concerts. The reggae style music they played was really catching on. In the 90's Mawg organized a music video shoot for his new song, "Waiting for the Aliens." This video was modeled after the movie "Close Encounters of the Third Kind" and included Jill's puppet Tri-Zorg the three-headed alien. His most recent album is called "Anchovy Picnic" and includes songs like 'Pick Yourself Up' and 'No One Left to Bust'. B-Dub now calls herself B-Wishes and is a singer-songwriter sensation on her own. Her tutoring of the Dome School music group really inspired the young students to sing beautifully. At each Holiday Bazaar in December, they can be heard singing and bringing tears to parent's eyes.

Some of the unsung musicians of Takilma are Pat M. on piano, Mikal M. on electric guitar, JD and Kim Smith who play in bands like The Plastic Onion in the Bay Area, Bruce M. playing original songs on folk guitar, Shabaka on drums, Tomas singing and playing guitar and drums at his Thursday night drum circle, Daniel S. on guitar and specializing in sound systems, Carol V. for her original songs and guitar, Terry L. for her ukulele, George S. on Banjo, Sparrow on accordion, Terry D. for his many years playing in bands and Libby for her original songs on guitar and piano. This is only scratching the surface of those not already mentioned, and I am sure there are more closet musicians than I can name and of course the young people who are starting their own music groups as well. One of the best of those new groups is the Rap group the Onieronauts, started by Patrick's son Shen and Kenny's son Tyrone.

Many people came up with revolutionary ideas to keep themselves busy. Radio Free Takilma was started with the desire to play music and keep people informed. You see after the Fire of '87 people started a phone tree to communicate and for emergency preparedness. The radio station performed that role. Beyond that people wanted to perform and play their music and have a forum for community discussion and creativity. It started small and ran for a few years as a pirate station before it was eventually busted by the FCC. People were using an empty slot on the FM dial which could only be heard in Takilma, and a continuous feed of live and DJ directed music of many genres, interviews, poetry, comedy and political satire was played.

DJ's like Little Sister, Mr. Unmentionable, Misty Rainbow, The Reverend El Sey, Miss Kitty, The Hurdy-Gurdy Man and the Spaceman were passionate about their shows and brought a wealth of music knowledge to the table. The station eventually moved to a new location and with the leadership of Leo the Spaceman, Lost Forest Recordings and small group of dedicated DJ's they started a legal station streaming live over the internet, which still exists to this day. It is known as Hope Mountain Radio. Please listen in at www.takilmafm.com

During a later period, the musicians of Takilma were developing relationships with the wider community. Robert H. said that "Jim N. used to rent the County Building every Tuesday night so various musicians from all over the Illinois Valley could play together. Out of that group, 3 or 4 music groups have formed. Those music groups now are very important in bringing people together."

Today Robert plays "Americana" style music with Doug, Walt and others in his group; East Fork. He is also a member of a new group called "Lonesome Road." The Chamber of Commerce started an annual Bluegrass Festival near Lake Selmac in 2004, and has invited groups like East Fork and Lonesome Road to have more opportunities to perform locally. "The evolution of the music in Takilma was really a big part of life here. We really dug playing together" said Robert. As he remembered, "There were so many talented musicians, and places we could perform." Recently East Fork, and many of the other music groups are planning to make a CD of the Illinois Valley sound.

Maya once said, "We built this city on rock and roll", referring to the numerous yearly benefits for the Takilma Community Building, Dome School and other worthy causes. She remembers, "We danced, oh did we dance, outdoors and at the Dome School." People lovingly gave of their time, food and talents to volunteer for these events which were known for their great music, fun and creativity. The Illuminated Fools, a giant puppet troupe created by Newman, were the rage of all the parties. In more recent years, Jill T's giant puppets, known as Coyote Rising have been bringing fun to most of the events. Takilma was known for its Mardi Gras Dance, Women's Café, Barter Faire, Halloween Dance, Holiday Bazaar, and Martin Luther King Day Dance, among others. Many of these benefits were supported by the great local music groups which I am sure donated much of their pay back to the community.

Another of the exceptional creations of the community was the Takilma Common Ground; a newsletter about and for the people, family, friends and supporters of Takilma. Created in 1990 by a small group led by Laurie P., Dave and Cathy H., Rachel G., and a few others; it was a hand written and illustrated journal of local interest and creativity. It was a good way for people to share what they were thinking and bring forth ideas and announcements to the residents. Many of the stories it featured were written by Robert and Delbert about early Takilma and their adventures. It has survived the years by being supported by its reader's subscriptions and is now under the umbrella of the Takilma Community Association.

Since the early 90's the internet has dramatically changed people's lives and allowed many to work at home. Other services for health care like naturopathy, massage therapy and acupuncture have thrived since 2006, in the old Takilma Clinic building, as a new generation of practitioners is working at the healing center again. Dr. Margaret, a naturopath, set up shop there shortly after moving to Cedar Gulch from Washington. She is joined by Louisa and Karen who do acupuncture and other healing arts. Other people are self employed and provide the services of accountants, tax preparers, nurses, seamstresses, computer technicians and handymen, to name a few.

One resident, Paula, learned to bake exceptional Danish pastries and makes a good living selling her goodies all around the valley. Another great baker, Kate D. is a first class chef and bakes scrumptious goodies and caters for large events from her home in Takilma. As if that were not enough she has gone on to become a Librarian and was recently elected to the Three Rivers School Board.

The community fortunately has supported a vigorous alternative economy of musicians, artists, farmers and craftsmen. This has encouraged new growth in the bridge between Takilma and Cave Junction, in which people are sharing their art and making their town a better and more vibrant place to enjoy. Artists like Mark and Beth make baskets from local trees, Dudley sculpts from local wood, Dave K. blows glass art, Libby weaves with natural yarns, Paco makes buttons, Marjorie sculpts and makes silver jewelry and Delbert makes pole and burl furniture, to name a few. Along that same line, Marjorie's straw-bale house looks like a work of art, and received an award from Josephine County for being the best alternative design. Marjorie can often be heard playing her flute around the valley.

An early Takilma music jam with Robert, Buckwheat
Bob and Flo Michels-photo courtesy of Robert Hirning

Robert and Charley playing music-
photo courtesy of Robert Hirning

PART 17

Clean up Challenges

T he challenges of inter-personal conflicts and differences might have taken some on an unexpected detour, and divorce may have broken up some alliances, but friendships and connections have rarely been broken. The dedication of the hippies to their little corner of the earth has been strong. Over the years, the difficult tasks of making improvements to old homes and buildings, and the daily struggle to survive and pay the bills were very hard, but the extremes of weather made things even worse. I suppose it was before most of the hippies arrived, but the flood of 1964, was supposed to have made the East Fork of the Illinois jump its banks and there was 40ft of water on Sauer's Flat. Two big freezes below zero degrees were in 1972 and 1989. Everyone remembers the year 1989 as the one where everybody's plumbing had to be repaired in the dead of winter.

After the Fire of '87, there was an appeal of the Environmental Assessment for the Longwood Salvage

Timber sale, which named Jonny K. and Pat M. as the plaintiffs. The Forest Service as part of its settlement to these landowners who were mainly affected by the fire, agreed to construct the Takilma Bike Path. There was a great deal of concern for the safety of people and their pets on the road with the logging and fire trucks. A Forest Service crew worked with community people who were hired to do much of the labor. The foreman of the crew was former Takilmanite John J. The Forest Service also got permission for easements and applied a layer of crushed granite to the surface of the path. In the end the Takilma Bike Path stretched from 4 Corners to Hogue's Meadow and provided a safe and enjoyable alternative to motorized travel throughout Takilma. Romain, a forest biologist from the Meadows said, "The Bike Path ended where the East Fork Illinois River Trail begins. The East Fork Illinois River Trail stretches all the way to Young's Valley in the Siskiyou Wilderness. So a hiker could start at 4 Corners and walk deep into the Wilderness and come out on the Klamath River."

It is quite thought-provoking to remember that some people did not always get along with Michael G. of the Treesort and went out of their way to make life difficult for him. One neighbor started to challenge the easement he shared with Michael by blockading the private driveway to Michael's back meadow. He also blocked off the access to a piece of a historical horse trail which went back to T.a.'s, the Farm and Hope Mountain. He did not like the fact that Michael's family and friends would cut through the back corner of his land so he covered the trail with slash, rocks, and broken glass. Michael finally took him to court, and sued him for blocking off his written easement. After that this same neighbor kept starting fights until he got Michael arrested, for alleged stalking and a vicious dog attack. The judge must have seen through that and Michael won the case and a $5,000 judgment, as well as a legal prescribed easement. The disgruntled neighbor had to cut down all his big trees to pay for the lawyer. He quickly sold his land and told everyone he was moving to Alaska to hunt bears.

It was due to this strange chain of events that Betsey N's family moved to Takilma, and bought this man's land. Betsey said, "We wanted to get the community back on track again, because we knew what a traumatic experience it had been for everybody. So we just decided we were going to be the peace keepers. So the first thing we did was we went up there and cleaned the community trail out completely from what was blocking it until there was only one tree left. So we sent down for Michael to come with his chain saw, and we had him cut the last tree out. Just trying to make things right again! T.a. was on the other end, and he opened up the other end and it was wonderful to just get that trail opened up again!" Betsey's family has welcomed a more peaceful atmosphere since then. With the advice of Romain, they were able to restore the natural meadow that used to grace their yard and to allow non-motorized travelers to use the community trail once again.

Many times hippies helped to clean up the earth when there was a need. Beginning with the clean ups of Hogue's Meadow, and the clean ups on Rough and Ready Creek, groups have formed to clean up the awful trash left on public lands by low lives and vandals. One recent group, calling itself the Friends of French Flat, has cleaned up massive loads of rubbish, dumped into and near the Logan Cut. Inspired by the leadership of Greg and Mary W.; the community rose to support their valiant efforts to restore the French Flat area, a beautiful lowland ecosystem.

Just two years ago, another group of various volunteers, took it upon themselves to clean up a piece of property near the corner of the TCA property, along the creek. This tiny bit of land had 2 trailers and an old mobile home abandoned on it, and attracted the homeless and other vagrants to hide there. The people were fed up with looking at that horrible sight, so they got permission from a Mr. H. and started a massive clean up, including recycling of any of the metals and other materials. As days went on, many from the community stopped to help or donate funds for gas money. Finally it was done and cleaned, and one man even stayed on over the summer to rake and clean all of the trash out of the creek. It was a labor of love, to know that the children would be safe walking around town again. Surprisingly, the real owner of the property, after hearing of and seeing the clean up, was so appreciative of the community of Takilma, that she promised to donate money to the Dome School and the Library.

Then just this last fall of 2012, the little red "Love House" in Takilma, where Otis lived and Ed Little Crow and Kitty lived before him, burned down. Tragically, it took his life, that Halloween night. Afterwards, the community decided that the sight was just too heart-breaking to live with and started a clean up of that place too. Today, the work is done, and the scars are healing over. People are envisioning just letting that land rest, and having it be an open space for those of us that are left to carry on life in Takilma. Someone remarked recently, "Otis' passing felt like the end of an era." Currently the Spiral Living Center is planning an Otis Jones Memorial Bike Ride, all the way to town, for the summer of 2013.

Takilma once had a sign at Four Corners, which said "Nuclear-Free Zone ~ Think Globally-Act Locally", and it reflected the general philosophy of the population. It was art donated by Jefry, but it was stolen, presumably by the same type of thieves that once stole the Angel Sculpture off of the Coffee Heaven roof in the middle of the night. These thieves favored stealing public art and bashing mailboxes. The long tradition of thievery in the Illinois Valley, started back in the 80's when the bronze plaque from the Waldo Township memorial marker was stolen. The people all over the valley were angry about that loss, and it as an issue brought people together, to protect a priceless piece of history. A replica plaque has recently been replaced on that marker by the E Vitus Clampus Organization, after people did fundraising to try to replace it.

Here is what is now says:

SAILOR'S DIGGINS

In 1852 English sailors jumped ship in Crescent City to go east in search of rumored gold strikes, and found "color" at what became known as Sailor's Diggins. By January 22, 1856 this had become the town of Waldo, the first territorial seat of Josephine County, with the Post Office established the same year. The town was named for William Waldo, brother of California Judge Daniel Waldo. With the stores, saloons, billiard halls boarding houses and hotels, a skating rink and a bowling alley, Waldo reached a population of 3,000, only 1,500 of whom were citizens, and 600 were "Celestials", Chinese who could not become citizens, or own gold claims or other property. Oregon's first water rights were established here making Waldo the hub of Oregon's first hydraulic mining industry. As the gold played out, many of Waldo's residents drifted away. In 1919 a land development company sold housing lots and began building a home which was never completed. In 1927 Waldo was leveled by the giant hydraulic mining water cannons of the placer mines. The dreams of its residents gone, now only the occupants of the hilltop cemetery remain to watch over the once-thriving community of Waldo, Oregon.

This plaque was placed on October 8, 2011 by the Umpqua-Josephine Chapter 1859 of the Ancient and Honorable Order of E Clampus Vitus, in cooperation with the Josephine County Historical Society.

The people of Takilma no doubt had their share of challenges over the last 40 years, but they always worked hard, and found solutions to better their lives and the lives of their community and now even their town; Cave Junction. People from Takilma that worked in the trades were creating inroads with the locals and being appreciated for their special talents and abilities. From Doug's Building Designs and abilities to be a "go-between" and mediate with the Building Dept, to Robert's dedication to the best in plumbing workmanship, to Charley's engineering of tree houses, and human-powered cars, to Mike M.'s muscle with the concrete, to Lance's woodworking, to Otto's car and pump repairs, to David's fertilizer and firewood deliveries, and many more industrious workers. It seems people really found their calling in Takilma.

Many bridges were built in the schools and other organizations, because the Takilma people were some of the best teachers they had. Takilma people like Alyce, Della, Sally C., Cathy and Bill D. and Trish C. were among the most favored teachers at Evergreen Elementary and Lorna Byrne Middle School. With Takilma people getting involved in town because of their children, it seemed that the lines were getting blurry; the hippies were fully part of the larger community. The talents and skills of some of Takilma's best and brightest were finally being noticed and appreciated by the general public. The old stigmas were melting away. As Alyce fondly remembers "People were surprised and told me, but you're just so nice!"

The community bulletin board in front of
the clean-up site-by Kindi Fahrnkopf

Otis's land after the clean up-the former site
of the "Love House" by Kindi Fahrnkopf

PART 18

Solutions and Economic Development

A
nother Takilma resident who found success after settling in the remote commune just over the border in California was Kenny H. He also found Sun Star from word of mouth, after hitchhiking up in 1974. After college and work down south he and his wife Marilyn at the time were able to keep their connection and eventually bought their first share in the alternative country club. This led to Kenny becoming a "serial entrepreneur" and buying a mobile coffee cart from John and River, named "On Common Grounds." His knowledge of the import-export business and Marilyn's experience from working at Hammer's Market and Captain Mike's Fish House, led them to buy the business. He gives lots of credit to Jeff and Karen of the Chevron Station for letting them open the Coffee Heaven Shop on the corner of their lot. It had a small shed which had previously been a kiosk for visitors. Marilyn took on the business and has created a beautiful oasis out of that shed and a place where rock work and botanical gardens decorate

the shady enclave of tables and a swing. Her success as a business owner by selling organic coffee and other drinks and products has been steady for the last 20 years.

Kenny continued working as a wood worker, making custom cabinets, shelves, etc. In 2010 after years of involvement with the Siskiyou Field Institute and their move to the Deer Creek Center, Kenny got recruited to the Board of the Illinois Valley Community Response Team. This group was formed from a Clinton era government grant to create one of 33 Enterprise Zones in Oregon which would help foster economic development. Over the years Kenny has worked with other community leaders, on the Siskiyou Community Health Center, the Airport Industrial park, the Family Coalition Building and many other projects. After the IVCRT changed into the Illinois Valley Community Development Organization, by forming a partnership with Rogue Community College, it opened a satellite office in the newly remodeled Kerby Belt Building. Now called the RCC Building, the Small Business Development Center helped people with a business incubator program and a revolving loan fund. Kenny has been instrumental in helping people start small businesses in the Illinois Valley.

The IVCDO helped broker a contract with the National Park Service, to run the Oregon Cave's Chateau restaurant and gift shop. It sells artwork and crafts selected from many local artists and employs people seasonally, thereby keeping those tourism dollars in the valley. The IVCDO is a real success story because it is the only one of those original

Enterprise Zones which is still functioning. Kenny is hopeful about the local economy because he sees "signs that property values are rebounding."

Kenny loves his work in the valley, but admits it has been challenging living so far out in the woods. He and his new wife Emily are able to spend more time doing the things they love these days. Kenny says, "Being able to get out in the winters and travel is what makes it all possible."

Kenny is the drummer for Altered States in his spare time and plays all kinds of percussion instruments. The types of music the group plays has changed over the years and now has a more Latin flair, with salsa and up tempo dance music added to the rock and roll. It has a decidedly new age, retro flavor these days. With Charley's guitar genius, Dave's bass and Donny's trumpet, they are one of the most popular bands in Southern Oregon and played two Mardi Gras gigs just recently. People wait all year to hear them perform outdoors at the Annual Sun Star Picnic; a benefit for Sun Star's fire prevention truck and equipment.

As people faced different challenges, they also created networks and friendships which helped them connect to the solutions. There was definitely a great feeling neighborly support given to local small businesses and organizations. In fact there were many opportunities available for people to diversify their income through arts, crafts, local foods, music and teaching their skills.

Other ways that people found involvement and solutions in Takilma was through bartering and sharing. They created and volunteered for events which supported the Dome School and Community Building improvements while allowing for an alternative economy to take root. They decided to make the events as fun and imaginative as possible, using the hippie ideals of solar energy, recycling and zero-waste among others. First an organization calling itself the Shining Stars, started having an annual festival every summer. In 2008, the Barter Faire Committee, (now known as Youth Empowerment & Support) took over and continued the 3 day music festival called Barter Faire which still is put on every year in the Illinois Valley. (The original Barter Faire started out in Ruch and Williams) This annual benefit for the Dome School also helps local business and tourism, bringing in hundreds of visitors every summer.

The Spiral Living Center has sprung up in more recent years to foster the growing home gardening and farming movement. To be able to produce some food locally has been the dream of many Takilma residents, who are working towards a more sustainable and self-sufficient community. Indeed the challenge of growing healthy organic gardens has been the life's work of many who settled here as part of the back-to-the-land movement.

Debbie L., the Director of the Spiral Living Center, started the small non-profit as a way to "live her dream." She explained how she and others, "wanted to help our community to attain self-sufficiency with permaculture, using lessons on creating a forest garden, with diverse interconnections, to support more than our human species. It is a way for us to give back." Her extensive home gardens are an example of people working hard at their dreams. One of the programs of the Spiral Living Center is called Toolshare and helps people donate, share and borrow tools which they need. One of those tools is an apple press which can quickly turn those excess apples into cider; a delicious reward for country living.

Debbie first moved here in 1987, to have her son Jacob and lived through hard times in a tent and a small Dome, before finding her own land. She started her small business, Siskiyou Mountain Herbs, using her lifetime of botanical learning and skills at organizing. She creates and preserves many different types of herbal and medicinal healing products which she lovingly crafts at her workshop. Not only does she grow many of the herbs she uses but she gathers many others and takes folks out to learn on herb walks and teaches classes.

If her wealth of knowledge doesn't keep her busy enough, she and her husband Steve also work on their "Frog Farm" where they raise organic goats, chickens and all of the by-products, like eggs, milk, meat and cheese. Debbie clearly is happy, even though she is often tired from working hard. "This is poor man's land. We can love it because we can choose it. I had to go through a journey of healing myself here, to make myself feel whole. I feel cradled by this little valley here." From the look on Debbie's face, one can see that she feels contented with her life in Takilma and has found great joy. The Spiral Living Center formed a group which puts on an annual Farm and Garden Festival in Cave Junction, to help people sell their produce and share skills, among other programs.

Altered States Band performing at the Mardi
Gras Dance-photo by Kindi Fahrnkopf

The Dome School with artwork by the
students-Photo by Kindi Fahrnkopf

PART 19

The Environmental Years in Takilma (Part 1)

The evolution and impact of the environmental movement in Takilma is explored in the next two chapters. In these two segments I used the full names of the employees and supporters of the Siskiyou Project; a non-profit organization.

The Siskiyou Regional Education Project, 1983-2013

The Siskiyou Regional Education Project was founded in 1983 in Takilma, Oregon. It started as a small but aggressive grassroots environmental group, which had organized around the Bald Mountain Road Blockade in the Kalmiopsis Wilderness. The two main founders of the group were Pedro Tama, a tree planter and forestry worker from the Forks of Salmon, and Lou Gold a former political science professor from Oberlin College in Ohio. These two men were drawn together by their mission to save what was left of Oregon's magnificent old-growth forests.

In 1983, Lou Gold met Pedro and others from Takilma at the first Bald Mountain Road Blockade into the Kalmiopsis Wilderness. Forest activists were calling for people to participate in the first non-violent blockade of a logging road being punched into the new wilderness, created in 1964. This led to six consecutive human blockades of the bulldozers building the Bald Mountain Road, 44 arrests, and eventually a legal victory which halted the construction entirely. The next week after his arrest, Lou was back on Bald Mountain and vowed to remain and bear witness to the attack on the forest and pray for its safety. He had bonded with many other young forest activists and had found an urgent mission in the protection of the few remaining ancient forests in southwest Oregon.

Lou Gold, had discovered the magic of a place called Bald Mountain, through which a line had been drawn between the Kalmiopsis Wilderness to the south and the remote roadless areas slated for logging on the north side. During his second summer, a series of ceremonies had been conducted and the Takilma Peace Circle dedicated Bald Mountain as a sacred place to pray for world peace. A group of friends had formed and were delivering food to Lou throughout the summers. Lou had been busy up on top of Bald Mountain cleaning up the debris and remnants of a fire tower which once stood there, and the Forest Service had allowed him to stay on as a special volunteer. His agreement with the Forest Service called for him to maintain the Bald Mountain Lookout Trail.

Lou, began his career as a "Storyteller" during those early years, and carved many beautiful walking sticks, which he gave as gifts to the occasional visitors. He created a sign which read: **Bald Mountain Sanctuary-Follow the Beauty Trail-Come in Peace**. By summer solstice, Lou and a few friends had built a "Medicine Wheel" at the barren top of the mountain, based loosely on the traditional Native American Medicine Wheel, a prayer circle marking the four directions with flagpoles. They spent 24 hours fasting and praying in the silence of the sacred circle. Lou had a vision of many prayer circles; places of power and renewal, which would be sanctuaries for those who love the earth and her peoples.

During the fledgling non-profit's early years, Pedro Tama, along with a talented group of young activists had begun to educate and inspire the local community about the activities in the "bio-region." The "tree-free*" Siskiyou Country Journal*, brought the new eco-politics into the small eco-communities of southern Oregon and Northern California. The journal provided a platform for Lou, and other writers to tell their stories, publish environmental analyses and appeal for public support of Lou's annual vigils on Bald Mountain. Then Lou got the idea to take his message on the road, and Marybeth Howell, of Portland, helped Lou organize a National Tour. Lou developed a slideshow and went to campuses across the nation, to generate over 3,000 letters in support of a Siskiyou National Park. The media had been calling Lou Gold the "hermit with the most frequent-flyer miles", but the Forest Service ignored the letters.

In 1987 dry lightning fires were ignited over southern Oregon, and started the Silver and Longwood Fires. Lou was driven out of his forest home on Bald Mountain and escaped through the Illinois River Canyon. Lou met many on his travels, including people in high places. He flew over the vast Kalmiopsis with Congressman Jim Jontz of Indiana, who as a member of the House Agriculture Committee, had become compelled to be a champion of Pacific Northwest forests. The Siskiyou Project was able to open an office in Takilma, in the former home of the Takilma People's Clinic, started by Dr. Jim Shames.

Lou Gold continued to travel and connect with other environmental groups such as, the Environmental Law Conference in Eugene, the National Wildlife Federation, American Lands Alliance and the Wilderness Society. Some interesting alliances were made and with the help of Dave Willis, Board member and wilderness guide, Bald Mountain camp became a meeting place for many powerful leaders in the movement. The massive fires had spared the Bald Mountain sanctuary, racing up the slope only to die out before reaching the top. The passion to protect the beloved Siskiyous was growing.

Throughout the 80's and 90's the journal also reported news of an annual 3 day "Bio-regional Conference", which united advocates for the area. The conferences were a fertile breeding ground for alliances, new campaigns and strategies to develop in the environmental movement. The young educational group had expanded by 1987, to host the 3rd annual Bioregional Conference at Humboldt State University, attended by 700 people. The *Siskiyou Country Journal* was 60 pages long, with 2500 copies per issue being sent out. In 1986, with help from the Oregon Natural Resources Council in Portland, the Siskiyou Project launched a campaign to protect much of the Siskiyou Wild Rivers area as a National Park, and garnered the support of Congressman Peter DeFazio.

In 1990, after proposing a study area for the bio-region the Smith River National Recreation Area was created but the Oregon side remained unprotected.

Since forest policies were the predominant issues, and several timber sales were being planned in and around the forest communities, the young non-profit organization, found itself drawn into activism to counter proposals to log, mine and spray toxic herbicides on federal lands. The Siskiyou Project began its Forest Watch Program and was successful in stopping timber sales along the East Fork of the Illinois River, and obtained a moratorium on herbicide spraying, through administrative appeals and direct action.

In the early 1990's the Siskiyou Project, having centered on the goal of permanent protection, and achieved the financial support of foundations through the work of early administrator Shel Anderson, hired a staff of dedicated workers. Cathy Hocker came on to manage the books, and Romain Cooper and Barbara Ullian laid down a conservation program. Kelpie Wilson crafted the newsletter, now called the "Voice of the Wild Siskiyou" and worked to fundraise and develop the network of supporters. Barry Snitkin and Deb Lukas began the process of local organizing. Steve Marsden took on the leadership role and took the conservation proposals to Washington DC, working with political leaders.

Lou Gold as Storyteller-photo courtesy of Lou Gold

The Bald Mountain Blockade-courtesy of Lou Gold

PART 20

The Environmental Years in Takilma-(Part 2)

The Siskiyou Regional Education Project, 1983-2013

In 1995, protests were planned against the Sugarloaf and China Left Timber Sales near the Oregon Caves National Monument. Hundreds of protesters were gathered to stop the logging trucks from entering the forest, and many were arrested one day including the Executive Director of the Siskiyou Project, Steve Marsden, Steve Jontz, Congressman from Indiana, Brock Evans of the Audubon Society and Charlie Ogle of the Sierra Club. Although the timber sales were later clear-cut, the media with a live CNN broadcast helped propel the event into the public arena and for the first time pictures of huge fir stump fields were published, to the horror of the public which believed that the national forests were protected. It became obvious that the biggest and the best trees were being harvested and the remaining forest was being degraded by the process. The Spotted Owl debate heated up and the controversy between loggers and forest guardians became a national issue. Meanwhile Siskiyou Project used the publicity to gather many more members and to expand its operations, in hopes of permanent legislative protection.

In 1997 the Siskiyou Project hosted its First Conference on Siskiyou Ecology, attended by 300 scientists, students, land managers and local citizens. The Siskiyou Field Institute was the idea of botanist Jennifer Beigel and as a result of her coordination, by 1999 provided the educational component of the Siskiyou Project's programs, with over 33 science-based field courses on the ecology of the Klamath-Siskiyou Bio-Region. The success of the Field Institute in the coming years, under the leadership of Sue Parrish, who expanded its programs, was so strong that the Institute eventually in 2004 was able to become its own non-profit organization, by partnering with Southern Oregon University and the River Network.

In 1998 the Siskiyou Project, along with partners at the World Wildlife Fund and leading scientists Dr. Reed Noss and Dr. James R. Stritcholt, of the Conservation Biology Institute produced the Klamath-Siskiyou Conservation Plan, a landscape level conservation biology assessment which would include comprehensive maps of the region, and its resources. The Siskiyou Project had also managed to secure Land and Water Conservation funds to buy out 2000 acres of mining claims, along the Wild and Scenic Chetco River, inside the Kalmiopsis Wilderness. By the next year, their massive public outreach campaign convinced the Forest Service to deny a large strip mine along Rough and Ready Creek, the most botanically diverse watershed in the State of Oregon. They also helped create a 1,162 acre Area of Critical Environmental Concern, called the "Redrock Rainforest" on BLM lands near the Redwood Highway.

In 2000, under the able and brilliant leadership of Kelpie Wilson, the Siskiyou Wild Rivers National Monument campaign was launched. Collaborating with the Soda Mountain Wilderness Council, led by Dave Willis, the Siskiyou Project supported both their own Siskiyou Wild Rivers campaign and the Soda Mountain National Monument campaign. Even with enthusiastic support from Interior Secretary Bruce Babbitt, the Siskiyou's were again second in line and not able to get the support of outgoing President Clinton. He created the Cascade-Siskiyou National Monument instead. At least the Siskiyous were getting some name recognition.

It was obvious then that more public and local support was needed to protect such a large landscape, however, due to Secretary Babbitt's support the Siskiyous were granted a two year moratorium on new mining claims. Siskiyou Project performed a field survey of mining damage on the area's rivers and streams documenting much damage. Photographer Barbara Ullian was able to document off-road vehicle damage to rare plant habitats and to help protect those areas. Special hikes and slideshows were held to draw attention to the need to protect the rare and endemic species of the eco-system.

The Voice of the Wild Siskyou's newsletter and the new www.siskiyou.org website, were used extensively to reach a network of members that Lou Gold had developed with this tour across America. The talented staff continued to bring attention to the issues through the skillful use of the media to affect public opinion.

Julie Norman, the former Executive Director of Headwaters, had been hired to create a Klamath-Siskiyou documentary to be aired on public television. Their filming schedule, included the talents of Ed Begley Jr. as narrator, and Martha Stewart, cooking salmon with Agnes Pilgrim, elder of the Rogue-Takelma Indians, for an upcoming TV special. Many other scientists and experts were interviewed as the film highlighted the regions many wonders. The film, in a slightly different format was aired on Southern Oregon's public television station.

In 2002, with the retirement of Lou Gold, a young enthusiastic campaigner was hired to replace him; Rolf Skar. Rolf, based in a small office in Portland, carried the word about the need to protect the Siskiyou all over Oregon and across the nation. His first summer the Kalmiopsis erupted in the Biscuit Fire of 2002, the largest fire in Oregon's history, and the Siskiyou Project responded by monitoring the fire and wildlands for the next several years. Ecologist Rich Nawa of the Siskiyou Project, worked with Conservation Directors Barbara Ullian and Romain Cooper to survey and monitor the activities in the fire area, creating a public outreach campaign against salvage logging, which studies had shown slowed the natural regeneration of the forests.

To help with educating the public, the Siskiyou Environmental Film Festival was held in Ashland each winter from 2002-2007. This program offered documentary films about the area and its ecology, fire science, forestry, restoration, wildlife and citizens. The festival, organized by Barry Snitkin, brought together the many groups and concerned citizens of the area to network with each other, and filmmakers from around the country. For the gala 20th Anniversary Festival, the special guest was Agnes Baker-Pilgrim, Elder of the Rogue-Takelma Indians, who spoke of her advocacy for Mother Earth.

A lawsuit to protect Oregon's cougar population was won by Siskiyou Project's staff attorney, Lori Cooper in 2004. An Economic Study of the Klamath-Siskiyou Bioregion by Ernie Neimi was produced by Siskiyou Project in 2005, helping to forecast the future change away from dependence on forest resources and jobs.

In 2006 the Siskiyou Project, opened an office in Grants Pass, and continued its public outreach campaign to gather support for legislative protection. Some of its original employees and board members have moved on, but the mission has not died, and is carried on by new activists with fresh energy. Recently, the Siskiyou Project merged with the Klamath-Siskiyou Wildlands Center of Ashland and continues to work for the permanent protection of America's precious ancient forests. www.kswild.org

Recently Lou Gold returned to Oregon from Brazil, his new home, to see old friends in the Illinois Valley. When asked what the environmental movement did right or wrong, he replied, "I don't think much about what's right or wrong these days, and the only thing I can say is, I can no longer depend on the same old assumptions that I used to use as a forest activist in America. The world is a different place today."

I was struck by the wisdom in those words; that we often grow older to find out how little we know about the world and its inhabitants and we are humbled and changed by that knowledge.

2013 marks the 89th birthday of Takelma Elder Agnes-Baker Pilgrim who has been a Voice for the Voiceless and a spiritual leader for many of the people of the Illinois and Rogue Valley's. I'd like to end this chapter with some excerpts of a speech she gave on her 86th Birthday, which I think perfectly expresses her environmental message to all of us.

Grandmother Agnes Baker Pilgrim said,

"Grandparents; you are the wisdom keepers. The rest of you are still in training, so lighten up. Getting old isn't for wimps is it? Us grandparents know that. I'm on roller blades, whether you can see them or not. I'm going all the time; to get home once in a while is a treat. Being this international Grandma isn't easy. I put in 10-14-17 hour days-try that when you're nearly 86 years old! It has been quite a journey; quite a story."

"We are being heard all over the world. I just got back from Australia, with the people over there from 39 countries at a conference. They are very concerned about our water all over the world. You should be too. Water is a precious commodity. Without water all life dies. Even a little blade of grass cannot live without water. Has anybody told you that you are all water babies? But then we grew up and we never took the time to bless the water. All of the green and air we breathe needs the water."

"Before when I was a voice for the voiceless, touring the world, all by myself, being this voice for the animal kingdom, (because they don't have a voice) for the air, and for the water and for the earth, I was a voice for the voiceless. So one time in the night I woke up and a voice told me that water could talk. Years went by until last year, I met Dr. Imerser Imoto, from Japan, the world famous scientist who had proven that water could hear. He wanted to know how I knew, and I said spirit told me. I knew we are all water babies, and water would call me as it has called my people for hundreds and hundreds of years. Without water we would all die."

"People are crying for water. Not just the humans but the animals too, and that big thing that happened down in Haiti—Pray for them. Send a message through the water in your body, to them down there. But we have to learn. I think our Mother Earth is angry at all of us, because in many places the water has dried up. Is she angry at us because we don't thank it? Is she angry because we don't talk to it? Is she calling it back to her? Because; we have become a people that forgot how to be grateful."

"Be that voice, talk to the water. We're all connected by water. We're all connected to each other. If we want peace in the world, we have got to learn to care for one another, speak well of each other, do something nice for someone else. If you want love, peace, joy and harmony-that's your inside job. I am a very grateful human being, passing on something you should be doing from now on. You should be thanking the water for sustaining your life."

This message from Grandma Agnes sums up her future hopes and prayers for the people of Takilma, and for the healing of the earth for future generations.

The Siskiyou Regional Education Project-Staff
and Board photo courtesy of Siskiyou Project

PART 21

The Hippies of Takilma—
Looking to the Future

Since 2008, things have changed quickly in Takilma, where people have always adapted and tried new things. The economy is more lucrative for ambitious entrepreneurs who are able to somehow make a living and work in the remote beauty of Takilma. Some of the hippie's children have stayed on and made homes for their young families. Their children now attend the Dome School. It is obvious that many appreciate the framework of community that exists there. Often they find housing close to home and are able to have the benefits of an extended family. Joya said, "I've appreciated a new group of 20-30 year olds taking ownership of the Dome School and taking over the fundraising and many other responsibilities." Joya added when asked about her future plans, "We're hoping to finish our years here on the land. We're hoping to bring another younger family in, to learn from us and take over."

Joya, who is still working for the Siskiyou Community Health Center, the IVHS Student Health Center, and the Josephine County Health Department, was honored by the State of Oregon in 2011 for being the "Family Planning Clinician of the Year." Joya exemplifies the loving Takilma spirit when she says, "I have much gratitude for three major influences upon my life. The first was my move to Takilma and the opportunity to join the Takilma Clinic's amazing staff and share in those exciting days of discovery and learning as a midwife in training. The second important influence upon my life was the birth of my son Danya, whose love carried me through many challenging years as a single mother and was instrumental in my growth and maturation. Danya continues to bring me joy, as does his son, Eli. The third important influence on my life is my husband Bill, who has been an incredible teacher to me about the wonders of the natural world, and who has provided me with continuous support and love through all of my life changes and challenges."

Robert, who has served as the Chairman of the Dome School Board for 11 years, said, "I am very hopeful the new generation of Takilma's young adults is going to take over and carry on the traditions and go on from where we started. My hopes are it will be different, but it will still be here. They've absorbed the spirit!" As Charley put it, "It looks like we are ready for another wave of consciousness." As an example of that he told me of Robin's daughter. "So, now Robin's daughter is going to SOU with a major in music; that's coming full circle!"

Delbert stresses that Takilma has assimilated into the rest of the valley, and contributed a great deal to its development. Robert who agrees with that said, "The spirit of togetherness has spread from Takilma to the wider valley. The most wonderful thing that has happened is that; if there is an 'us and them', now the Illinois Valley **is** 'us'."

Laurie P., who now lives at the coast, still visits Cedar Gulch often. Laurie says, "I still love coming to Takilma. It now feels like a retreat, so quiet and beautiful when I get to the end of the road. When I return to Cedar Gulch I cherish the darkness, clear drinking water, stillness and of course good friends—there is nothing like old friends that you raised your children with, grew up with and created a whole community complete with a school, a medical clinic, a work co-op and a food co-op. We had it all! From vision to reality! I feel blessed I was able to work at the Dome School, the Takilma Food Co-op, Green Side Up, volunteer at the Takilma People's Clinic and be a part of the staff of Common Ground. Being involved and a part of all the different entities helped me feel very connected with Takilma. It was a wonderful 30+ years!"

Mark K. from the Meadows remarked about the current state of Takilma, "Life's gotten easier for everybody. It's a combination of enjoying the fruits of your labor and a pot economy which some people are taking advantage of. People are going to need to find other ways to make a living. When the economy goes down the tubes, people help each other more. When people are dirt poor they get together and help each other out." Looking towards the future, Mark is sure some form of community will survive in Takilma. He says, "The TCA is holding six parcels of community land for all. At least the land will be here." Surely the hardy residents of Takilma see their place on earth as a continuous home for a new generation of young people to survive in; in fact they see it as an example of a successful model for other communities as well.

One might ask was the hippie experiment successful? Did they live up to their ideals? Is the dream still alive? Well let's start with what those hippie ideals were.

1) Environmental Activism-trying to save the world's forests, oceans, rivers, intact eco-systems and indigenous peoples. Promoting alternative and renewable energy sources and a return to local, organic food production. Living simply on the land and caring for the ecological well-being of all living things. Loving nature.

2) Pollution Activism-warning of the threats of chemical and petroleum pollution causing widespread damage and disease. The promotion of recycling, reducing and reusing as a way of life. The protection of the ocean and all of the world's creatures and a reverence for clean water, by the preservation of local water supplies and by the avoidance of all pollutants. Leaving less of a footprint.

3) Lifestyle Activism-leading the world in culture, styles, music, arts, alternative health practices, and the legalization of Marijuana. Living free.

These were the ideals of my generation; the things that united us to a cause greater than gaining wealth, fame and possessions in the material world. Hippies led the way perhaps without meaning to, but they set examples which doubtless influenced and impacted people far more than they were likely to admit. So the evolution of American history was the back drop to their quest for individual freedom and a new kind of collective creativity and cooperation.

I've got nothing but the history I've set down here to base my conclusions on, but my heart tells me that yes, the hippie experiment was successful in creating an alternative community in the foothills of the Siskiyous. And yes, they did live up to their ideals of loving the earth and protecting the land, air and water, living simply in a natural, organic and renewable way, and working in teams to build a sustainable community. They worked hard to use the democratic system to build consensus and alliances and oppose oppressive laws and actions. Their dedication to creating the structure and framework that could stand the test of time will certainly benefit the next generation. They fought for their own freedom and the natural world around them with ingenuity, persistence and courage. They did not always like or agree with each other, but they still communicated with openness and accepted and tolerated each others differences. They created a community in the true sense of the word; not a town with a gas station and post office, but a community of like minded souls, who were fully appreciating their lives together in such a beautiful and unique place. So yes, the Takilma dream is still alive, even as the community is changing very quickly and who knows what will come of it. I for one think it will be an example of sustainable living in the future.

Solutions have always been found in Takilma by people working together. When asked what were some of the greatest achievements of Takilma, Robert reflected that, "Over the years we have demonstrated our abilities to be leaders for positive change." When asked what **his** biggest accomplishment was, he looked down humbly and said, "I've learned so much here that it's more about what was contributed to me, than the other way around. I'm having the best time of my life-I'm free from all the struggles. All I hope for my future is to be buried up in those trees." as he pointed lovingly into the forest above his house.

In 2008 Robert refinanced his house and set out on a fantastic rail journey with his long term friend Donalee. Needing to fulfill a lifelong dream they boarded the Trans-Siberian Express and rode 12 days from the Sea of Japan to the Baltic (with a side in and out of Mongolia along the way), 9000 miles across Asia and European Russia. Robert said he wants his headstone to read, "There isn't a train I wouldn't ride, no matter where it's going" from a poem by Edna St. Vincent-Millay.

Charley, looking around at all the cars he has built, summed it up by saying, "What's special about Takilma is you don't have to take the standard prescription, you can make you own medicine." His unique inventions all around him seem to illustrate Charley's vision of a better world and his gifts to future generations.

Michael G. thinks Takilma, "Is still on an upward trajectory, There's a whole new generation now. It's still a healthy and vibrant community. Potentially it could explode into hyperspace. It all depends on what people do." Michael is an inspiration to many people, who also hope to find a way to make money without cutting down the trees.

Doug and Alyce were both lucky to have their parents move to the Illinois Valley during their later years. Their parents made many friends and enjoyed being able to be close to their children and grandchildren at the end of their lives. Doug said, "What is exciting to me is that the valley is continuing to be multi-generational." They can now easily adjust to being the elders in their family.

His neighbor, Sue agreed, saying that, "It just seems right for me to be doing this here. To be able to come home and walk to the river is what makes it all possible. Just to have that peace, that many people don't have, is a blessing! My grandchildren love to come here and visit. Every time I see them, they always ask me to tell them stories of what it was like."

Sheila, now retired with her husband Kerry, concludes that, "I feel like I have more than I can imagine. I have everything. For me one of the best things we did was we were teaching ourselves how to do sustainable living, without hurting the land, and being on the highest possible spiritual level. And we were constantly debating that issue, and I love that!" Kerry, who runs a business called Renewable Energy Systems, since 2003, designs and installs solar and hydro systems, so he can address many of those issues for the people in Takilma and the IV who want alternative energy. He jokes that, "Yes, you can go on vacation somewhere, to someplace that's supposed to be paradise; but THIS is paradise!" Sheila is content to enjoy her time, free of responsibilities. She adds that, "I am living the dream of my life! I've been into art all my life, but I had to be a weekend artist. Now I have a two acre art garden and all these sculptures are mine and I paint. It's been amazing to actually have the time to paint."

Jake feels quite content to be back home in Takilma, "I'll be 64 this year, and now *this* has become my job. These are the years I can finally live the life that I thought I was going to live at the Farm all those years ago. It's wonderful!" Jake and his new wife Carol are able to create beautiful gardens and help teach the younger generation, who've moved to the Farm, their knowledge and skills.

Delbert and Helen are quite happy living out their lives in the cradle of Takilma. They describe their greatest joys as the ones of being close to their large extended family. Their children still appreciate having grown up so free and uninhibited in such a beautiful place. Delbert attributes his long marriage to Helen with, "We had six kids, we were too poor to live separately, and the kids made great marriage counselors." Delbert, now a respected furniture artist, creates beautiful, sturdy furniture which graces businesses like Taylor's Sausage in Cave Junction. He and Helen live at a slower pace today, but seem to always have a mellow, cheerful smile on their faces. They have really found true happiness in Takilma.

The love and devotion people feel for their homes and families in Takilma is not surprising to me, but to anyone else, I'm sure they would look in from the outside with bemused astonishment at the hippie survivors who still call this place home. They might wonder what it was that kept them here. Love I say, it was all about love and peace.

Sheila and Helen: the heart and soul of Takilma.
Photo Courtesy of Delbert Kauffman

Charley with his Human-powered car-
Photo by Kindi Fahrnkopf

Robert and Donalee on the Trans-Siberian
Railway-photo courtesy of Robert Hirning

Delbert and Helen on their 50th Wedding Anniversary-
photo courtesy of Delbert Kauffman

CONCLUSION AND COMMENTS

I dedicate this book to all of the hippies from Takilma who have passed on already, such as Michael Dowling, Cathy Hocker, Patrick Farley, Alice Hestad, Brett Matusek, Gilbert, Redman, White Fox, James Barry, Joe Patton, Mark Rehmar, Steve Wireman, Kitty and Otis Jones and Lane Cosner. They all loved Takilma.

A late addition to this list is Jim Rich who passed peacefully from this earth on June 24, 2013. He was in many ways a leader and a founder of Takilma, who lived at the center of town and who gave freely and lovingly of his skills as a blacksmith, farrier, fireman, sailor and musician. His unique life was an example of all the best of our hippie ideals and he really lived them. He will be greatly missed as he was loved and respected by everyone. His was a life well lived.

Our generation is getting older as many of the early hippies are reaching the 80 year mark, and facing their mortality. That is why I have taken this opportunity to record the history of this place and its people. The younger ones of us are going into our 60's and taking on the challenges of aging and the changes which we are bound to embrace with fortitude and grace. It is with pride and gratitude that I have written this account of my community, which has entrusted me their stories and memories.

I wish to thank the many people who have generously given of their time and energy to give me interviews and photos for this book. Their knowledge and willingness to tell me about the things that happened made this book possible, and enjoyable to write. I have learned so much and found so many different viewpoints which helped me in my journey to express things "from a hippie point of view." One thing is truly paramount to all of my generalizations; that the hippies just wanted to be left to live in peace. Peace was their mission and their overriding commonality. Their failure to achieve peace in the political arena led them to drop out to find out if living in peace was truly possible. So their stories attest to their quest for peaceful, harmonious lives.

In my attempt to genuinely and fairly portray the population of "hippies" in Takilma, I was often at a loss for words, for I am one of them. I didn't want to label, sugar-coat, generalize or make sweeping assumptions about the people or events, which perhaps could be discredited by some who say I am looking through rose-colored glasses, so to speak. I did not knowingly misrepresent the truth and I apologize if there if are any fallacies. I have worked to check and correct my mistakes. I hope I have not been party to any judgments upon anyone. I hope I have not offended anyone by leaving their story out or in. For purposes of my format and length, I could not cover all of the 400 or more amazing people who've made the history of Takilma so interesting and diverse. (The official population of adults polled by the TCA in the year 2000 was 221.)

I cannot claim to be unbiased; I can only put forth my best efforts as a writer. My disclaimer is this is by no means exactly chronological or factual. Accuracy cannot be verified, nor can the names and identities of any of the parties. I have attempted to protect the privacy of my subjects by using only their first or nicknames, unless they were a public figure. I hope my readers will take this with a grain of salt and a pinch of humor. It is in the spirit of respect and love that I do speak of my community, which I love dearly.

In parting I will share the photo of Captain Jim aboard his beloved sailing ship. Sail on, dear friend!

Thanks to all who let me into their hearts and homes. It has been a long, strange trip!

In Peace and Love,
Kindi Fahrnkopf
Takilma, Oregon

Captain Jim Rich, with his crew on the sailing ship
"The Royaliste" Photo courtesy of Jim Rich

INTO THE MYSTIC

When one thinks of Takilma,
one thinks of mythical times
In the history of Hippiedom
Times when people were young and reckless,
When they challenged the system,
by the way they looked,
Behaved, spoke out and demonstrated.
It was a happening
And legends were born in the making.
If you made it through one winter in Takilma,
you could assume
You had made it.
My first winter I made it through
John Lennon's assassination
And I was back to the land.
There was such a weird, hallucinatory
vibe floating around
You could get caught up in inner
and outer encounters
With the truth you thought you could hide,
and be lost for days
There was a void waiting
to be succumbed to
And the only glue to hold you together
were others in the circle
Everyone was their own legend
and we lived for the now
I lived out my fantasies here
along with others in the tribe,

And I consider them my family now,
because we made it together
All the Jim's were the doctors, teachers,
blacksmiths, cobblers and woodsmen
All the Michael's were the musicians, actors,
tree planters and concrete builders
And most of them had to change their names
and others were known for their names
Like Delbert, Pradip, Paco, River,
Sitting Dog and Billy WooWoo.
Everybody had crazy people living next door
and seemed like everybody
Changed their names to avoid confusion,
or because they were outlaw legends
Funny how we had to name ourselves
and identify who we were.
A Nuclear Free Zone, a Community.
(Not a town with a gas station and post office.)
We worked hard and partied hard
and money manifested
and projects manifested
From wild parties we manifested
all we needed in our Community Building.
There were melodramas, drug wars,
shootings, rip-offs and drunken orgies
But there was also love, cooperation, dancing,
playing, gardens and children laughing
And more babies being born at home
and trees planted and families merging
There were secret gardens guarded,
high up in the hills
And late night negotiations, in smoke filled rooms,
where deals went down

And weird friends from out of town,
who came and never left, at the Green Bridge
Every day, living in their RV in your yard
for months on end, everybody was stoned
And more people fell apart,
divorced and found new love in Takilma.
Some left and never returned:
some moved over to Ashland and Eugene.
Some left for the tropics every winter
and became perennial travelers,
others stayed
The waves of change blew hard in Takilma
and there was always a threat to
unite us as we got older with struggles
and slowed down, some of us survived
Some went deeper into their worlds,
becoming eccentric recluses
Others went out into the community and got a job
Others created saleable merchandise and crafts,
businesses, art and music
We used out talents to weave
the fibers of a self-supporting community
Which gave each individual
a respected place in the fabric
However unique,
they were considered to be valuable members
Of Takilma, the land of the Takelma Indians before us.
It is a place of exceptional beauty
and harshness too,
As the Siskiyou Mountains are rugged and forbidding,
With many strange plants inhabiting
steep canyon rivers and forestlands
It's like going down a road that has an end

and it's a dead end
In a borderland that's Takilma;
it's not a place for people just passing through
It's a place to go when you want to retreat
from the world and where it's going.
You get grateful to be here and loving the peace.
That's when you've made it.

By: Kindi Fahrnkopf 1984

LIST OF
REFERENCES

"Takilma; Where a Dream of the 60's never died", by Rick Rubin and Photographs by Dana E. Olsen. The Sunday Oregonian magazine; Northwest. 2-15-90

"Standing Out, Fitting In" written by Beth Quinn, Sunday Medford Mail Tribune, 8-17-97

"Thousands of Freaks Blaze Oregon Trail" by The Oregon Journal, 8-5-1972.

"Oregon Town has Saucer Pad" by Marge Davenport and Rolen J. Crick, The Oregon Journal, 8-12-1972.

Reference to Rainbow Bob, by Paul McComber, Grants Pass Daily Courier, 1974

"Medicine Man" by Howard Huntington of the Grants Pass Daily Courier.

"Sort of a grand social experiment", by Shaun Hall of the Grants Pass Daily Courier.

"Times Mellowing Hand Touches Takilma" by Barbara Hahn and Paul Fattig, Grants Pass Daily Courier, 8-25-1990

Siskiyou Community Health Clinic "still for everybody." By Patti Richter Grants Pass Daily Courier 2-26-2009

"Golden Days and Pioneer Ways" by Ruth Pfefferle, Published by Bulletin Publishing Company, 1977.

Website for Agnes Baker-Pilgrim, www. agnesbakerpilgrim.org

Website for www.takilma.org and www.takilmafm. com

Cover photo by Joya Feltzin: Downtown Takilma and Hope Mountain taken from the Downtown Overlook.

Back Cover Photo by Jim Shames-The Takilma Community in 2004

This and other photos of early Takilma were previously published in a book of photographs, by Jim Shames, Magic Forest Farm and Friends.

"Magic Forest Farm and Friends—40 years of magic (1968-2008)" by Jim Shames and others in 2008.

The files and photos of Robert Hirning regarding the history of Takilma.

The newspaper archives of the Illinois Valley News

ABOUT THE AUTHOR

Susanne Kindi Fahrnkopf

The author at home in Takilma.

Susanne Kindi Fahrnkopf (far-en-kof) was born in Germany and grew up in Southern California, where she studied English Literature at Santa Monica City College. A poet and flower child of the 60's; Kindi moved to Cave Junction in 1979 with her husband and two little children to open the Cave's Cobbler shoe repair and Birkenstock shop. Since then she has raised four children in Takilma and works as a Bookkeeper. Here is her off-beat account of the history of Takilma. She explores the people, places and stories which have made her small alternative community a unique and exceptional place to live.

Kindi has been published in seven Poetry anthologies: *The Leaves of Autumn* 1983, *Spring Symphonies* 1985, *Day's of Future's Past* 1989 by the National Library of Poetry, *Poetic Voices of America* 1998 by Sparrowgrass, *Twilight Musings* by The International Library of Poetry in 2005, *"Sights Unseen: A Door to Enter"* by Eber and Wein Publishing in 2010 and again in *Best Poets of 2011.* Her first self-published book; *Siskiyou River Reflections* is a collection of her favorite poems inspired by her life in the community of Takilma in the heart of the Siskiyou Mountains.

Other accomplishments include writing a piece on the Siskiyou Project for the Oregon Encyclopedia website and re-writing a family memoir. Kindi compiled, edited and printed her father's autobiography, called "Wanderer Between Two Worlds", by Henry G. Rittenhouse in 2002.